Machine-Stitched
Cathedral
Stars

SHELLEY SWANLAND

Martingale™
& COMPANY

D1314570

Dedication

To the stars of my universe
My children: Rebecca, Sybill, Raymond, and Valerie
My grandchildren: Kelby and Kyler

CREDITS

President . . . . Nancy J. Martin
CEO . . . . Daniel J. Martin
Publisher . . . . Jane Hamada
Editorial Director . . . . Mary V. Green
Managing Editor . . . . Tina Cook
Technical Editor . . . . Karen Soltys
Copy Editor . . . . Liz McGehee
Design and Production Manager . . . . Stan Green
Illustrator . . . . Laurel Strand
Cover Designer . . . . Stan Green
Text Designer . . . . Trina Stahl
Photographer . . . . Brent Kane

That Patchwork Place® is an imprint of Martingale & Company™.

Machine-Stitched Cathedral Stars
© 2001 by Shelley Swanland

Martingale & Company
20205 144th Avenue NE
Woodinville, WA 98072-8478 USA
www.martingale-pub.com

Printed in Hong Kong
06 05 04 03 02 01   8 7 6 5 4 3 2 1

MISSION STATEMENT

We are dedicated to providing quality products
and service by working together to inspire creativity
and to enrich the lives we touch.

Library of Congress Cataloging-in-Publication Data

Swanland, Shelley.
   Machine-stitched cathedral stars / Shelley Swanland.
      p.   cm.
   ISBN 1-56477-370-1
   1. Patchwork—Patterns.   2. Machine sewing.
3. Machine quilting.   4. Star quilts.   I. Title.

TT835 .S8597 2001
746.46'041—dc21

2001034299

Contents

Introduction

I HAVE ALWAYS admired Cathedral Window quilts. I collected books and articles about them but could never finish one. So, in the summer of 1998, I was surprised when, in the middle of the night, an idea hit me. Basing my idea on the method used to make a three-dimensional Bow Tie block, I devised a way to make Cathedral Window quilts completely by machine. *Machine-Stitched Cathedral Windows,* my first book, was published a year and a half later. The response to my technique has been terrific, so I continue to develop new designs using the same basic methods. This book is a result of that effort.

Stars are one of my favorite patchwork designs, but they were nonexistent in Cathedral Window quilts until now. In this book, you will find twelve Cathedral Window Star blocks and twelve quilts based on those blocks. I think they are a lot of fun and exciting to make and hope you'll enjoy them, too.

I admit that at first glance this technique seems complicated, but it is actually quite simple. Take your time, start with a simple block, and, I promise, the light-bulb will go on once you sit down and stitch your first Cathedral Star block.

PART ONE
General Instructions

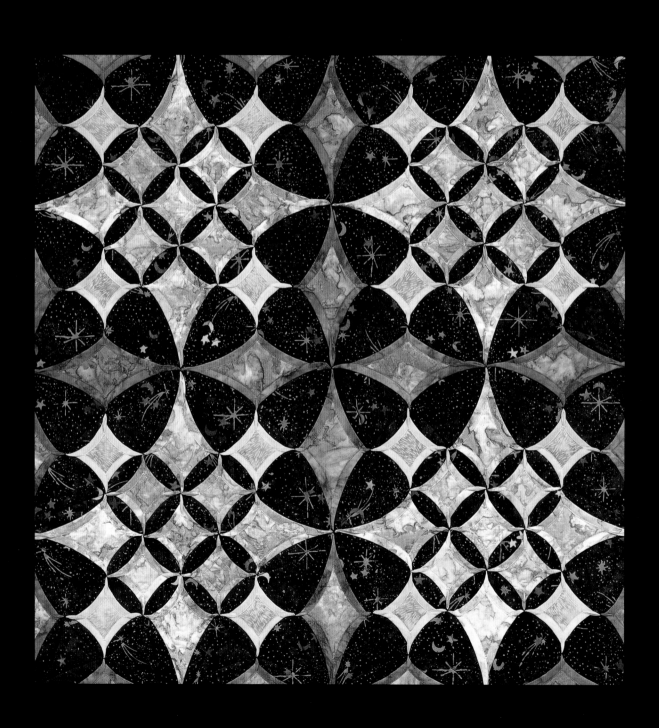

A LL OF THE blocks and quilts in this book are assembled using the same basic techniques and components. Whether your design starts with squares, diamonds, or kite shapes, the seams of the *window frames* are machine sewn into the *foundation,* an underlying grid that forms the entire quilt top. This top is then layered over the batting and backing. During basting, the *windowpanes* are positioned over the window frames, and the edges of the window frames are then folded over the raw edges of the windowpanes, tacked in place, and quilted by machine. Because this method is quite different from stitching regular patchwork, it is very important that you read through all of the general instructions before you begin any of the blocks or quilts in the book. Once you understand the basic concepts and try just one block, you'll find making any of the projects in the book to be successful and rewarding.

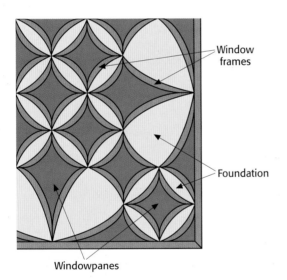

Window frames

Foundation

Windowpanes

Cutting the Pieces

EACH OF the projects in this book contains a cutting chart that tells you specifically what to cut. I recommend using a rotary cutter to do as much of the cutting as possible. When cutting squares or rectangles, it's the quickest and easiest way. However, many of the pieces in Cathedral Window Star quilts are not square or rectangular and require a little more ingenuity when it comes to using a rotary cutter. You'll find instructions with each quilt project that detail the cutting sequence so you can make the most efficient use of your fabric and cutting time.

The grain lines are indicated on all the patterns. Pay particular attention to the grain lines of the window frames. The frame edges will be folded over the windowpanes so they must be cut on the bias; otherwise, they won't stretch and lie flat. Since the windowpanes are purely aesthetic, they can be cut any direction that gives the look you want. When cutting the foundations and frame pieces, it's accuracy that's important. If the window-frame pieces are just a little larger than their patterns, you will be catching the seams.

Copy the patterns for your project onto template plastic. Follow the order of cutting given in the cutting chart for the least amount of waste. I recommend rotary cutting a strip and then cutting the individual pieces from there, when possible. You can cut several layers at a time; just be sure the blade in your cutter is sharp. (If you have to press very hard to make a cut, or the cutter is skipping over some threads, it's time to change the blade.)

Place the template on the strip and mark all edges with a sharp pencil, nesting the pieces whenever possible. Cut all outer edges with the rotary cutter if possible. You'll need to cut the inside angles with scissors.

Following are some additional helpful cutting tips:

+ Cut only the number of pieces specified for your project. The extra fabric is often used for other parts of the quilt.

+ When cutting right- and left-hand pieces, you need to alternate the right and wrong side of the fabric or flip your template and cut them individually. If you're cutting in layers, you can fold the fabric right sides together and cut both a right- and left-hand piece simultaneously.

+ Cut all foundation and frame pieces needed for your project before starting to sew.

+ You can wait until the top is assembled to cut the windowpanes. You might want to audition the fabrics once the frames are sewn together before you make your final choices.

Making the Foundations and Frames

To make a Cathedral Stars quilt, you'll be working in a grid format on foundations. Individual window-frame units are stitched together in a grid, much like patchwork blocks are laid out in a grid of rows and columns to form a quilt top.

Three window-frame shapes are used interchangeably in all of the designs in this book: square, kite, and diamond. When the quilt grid is made from a combination of rectangles and squares or a combination of different-size squares, diamond- and kite-shaped window frames are formed.

The method for constructing all window frames is basically the same. Only the length of the seams varies. Whether you're making a square frame or a diamond frame, four seams will meet beneath each full frame in all of the projects in this book.

Stitching the Seams

In general, seams are sewn as you would sew set-in seams, starting and stopping ¼" from the edges and backstitching at the beginning and end. However, you may find when assembling the frames that if you start ⅜" from the edge, it is easier to press the finished frame. The other exception is for edge frames. For these blocks, you need to sew the seam all the way to the outer edge.

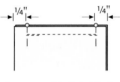

Seam used to join blocks

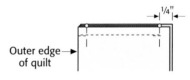

Seam used at quilt edges

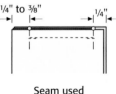

Seam used to construct frames

Assembling the Frames

You can approach the sewing sequence of the seams in these designs in several ways. I find that it's most helpful to work through the methods that follow with some sample foundation and window-frame pieces. Many of my students experience an "aha" moment as they make these samples. Once you are familiar with the technique, then the sewing sequence is up to you.

Sewing Square Frames

Option 1: Working around the Block

1. Using the frame and foundation square sizes required for the Floating Star block on page 25, cut at least one strip of fabric for each.

2. Start with four small square foundation pieces and one square frame. Fold the square frame in half, wrong sides together, forming a rectangle. With the short end up and the raw edges to the left, place the rectangle between two foundation pieces, right sides together. Line up the upper edge and left-side raw edges. The foundation pieces will extend ¼" from the frame fold on the right-hand side. Pin through all four layers on the fold and ¼" to ⅜" from the left side. The larger allowance at the start of each seam will help with the pressing.

3. With the fold of the frame facing you, backstitch to the first pin, then stitch up to the second pin, using a ¼" seam allowance. Take one stitch over the pin and backstitch.

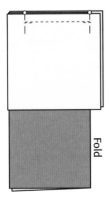

4. Rotate the block counterclockwise and open it out so you can see the wrong side of the frame fabric. Fold the lower right corner of the frame up to the seam's upper edge. Lay a foundation square on top, matching the four corners. Pin and stitch as shown in step 3.

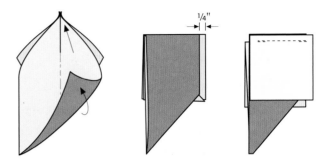

5. Repeat the rotating, pinning, and sewing process for the third seam.

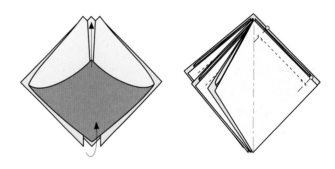

6. Bring the unsewn edges of the first and fourth foundation squares together, keeping the folded edge of the foundation square to the right as shown. Stitch as shown in step 3.

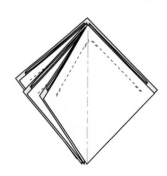

7. Now flatten the four foundation squares. This will pull the frame block into a square, set on point, with folded bias edges. Turn it over to see the four-square foundation grid.

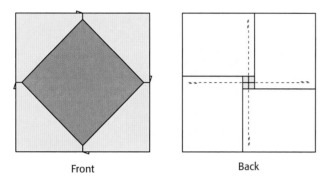

Front   Back

Option 2: Sewing Opposite Seams

1. Referring to steps 2 and 3 of Option 1 on page 9, stitch one window frame between two foundation squares.

2. Repeat step 1 to sew the remaining two foundation squares to the opposite end of the frame piece.

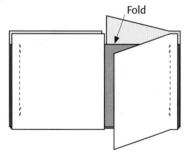

Fold

3. Grasp the seam allowances and push them together as shown until they meet. Pin the raw edges together.

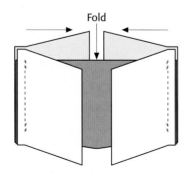

Fold

4. Sew the remaining seams individually, backstitching at the beginning and end of the seams. Do not sew across the center seam.

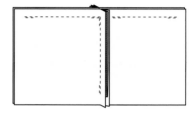

5. Open the unit and press the seams flat. It will look exactly like the completed unit shown in Option 1, step 7.

Attaching Additional Square Frames

Once you have completed a window-frame unit, you can begin attaching additional frames to build the interior portion of your quilt. The frames that make up the outer edges and corners of the quilt top are added later (see page 13).

1. The two raw edges of each individual foundation square will be stitched to an adjacent frame. Start in the upper left corner of your assembled frame unit. Fold a new frame square in half, wrong sides together, and lay it on the frame block, aligning the fold with the center seam allowance and the raw edges with the left side of the completed block. Lay a foundation square over the frame fabric; pin and sew as described earlier.

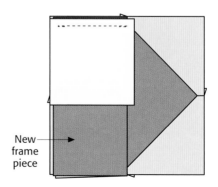

New frame piece

2. Work around this frame in the same manner as before until all four seams are sewn. Additional frames will be added in the same manner, based upon the individual quilt diagram and project directions.

3. Once you have added two frames to two adjacent corners of the original frame, you can add a frame to each of the corners to create a five-frame unit.

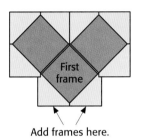

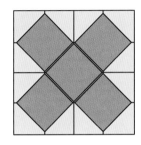

Add frames here.

4. Or you can add one frame between the second and third frames to create a four-frame unit. Since two foundation squares are already sewn onto the unit, you'll only need to add two more.

Add frame here.

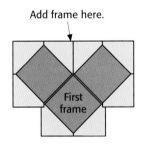

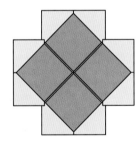

5. Another approach for a four-square frame unit is to sew the first seam of four frames, one at a time, and then add two foundation squares to finish each square frame. The choice is yours!

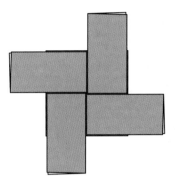

Kite Frames

While cutting kite-shaped frames is a little more time-consuming than cutting squares, their elongated shape makes wonderful star points. The units are assembled in much the same way as square units.

Sewing Kite Frames Using Foundation Rectangles

In the quilt blocks and projects in Part Two, beginning on page 22, each kite frame uses two small foundation squares and two rectangles. You can stitch the block using either Option 1 or Option 2 as described earlier. The long seams of the frame will be sewn between the long seams of the rectangles.

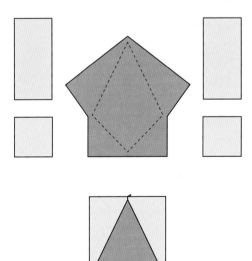

Sewing Diamond and Kite Frames Using Large Foundation Squares

For the blocks and projects in Parts Three and Four, beginning on pages 42 and 64 respectively, large and small foundation squares are combined to create the designs. The larger squares replace the rectangles, creating open space in the design.

The long sides of the diamond and kite frames match the sides of the larger foundation squares. Again, you can use either sewing method—Option 1 or Option 2—to make your units.

Each frame can be sewn individually, or the four longer seams that come together in the center of a block can be sewn first.

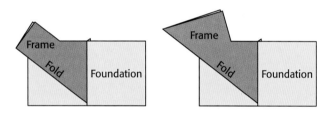

The shorter side seams use only half of the larger foundation squares. Just sew to the fold of the frame and backstitch, leaving half the seam open. A second frame will be sewn to the remaining part of the seam later. This same situation occurs when the blocks are finished without edge and corner frames in multiple-block quilts.

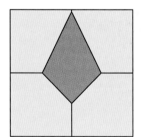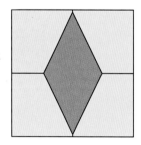

Sometimes it's possible to sew the entire seam at once. Place the two folded frames with folded edges butted together; pin in place. Stitch from one edge to the other through the frame folds, backstitching ¼" to ⅜" from each edge.

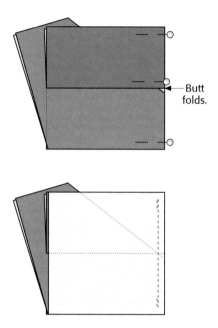

When the directions call for two small foundation squares on one side and a large foundation square on the other, sew the seams separately.

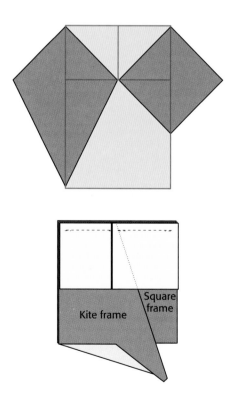

Finishing the Edges

No matter which option you use for sewing the foundation and frames together, all of the open seams on the edges of the quilt need to be sewn. At the edges, the foundation pieces will capture only one seam of the frame piece.

Edge Frames

1. Fold the edge-frame piece in half, wrong sides together. Lay the folded piece on top of the quilt, with the fold against a seam that runs parallel to the edge, matching raw edges.

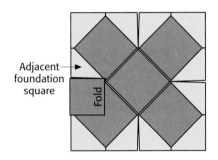

2. If there is an adjacent foundation square as shown above, fold it over the edge-frame square, right sides together. Stitch from the fold all the way to the opposite edge, back-stitching at the beginning and end of the seam.

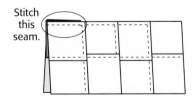

3. If there is no adjacent foundation square, add a foundation square and sew the seam as described in step 2.

4. Open out the edge frame and finger-press it in place. The folded edges nearest the raw edge should cross adjoining folds and seams. Stitch along the raw edge ⅛" from the edge to hold the layers in place; avoid seam allowances by lifting the presser foot and hopping over them.

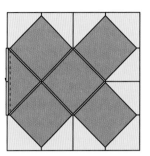

Corner Frames

You'll need to choose the type of corner frame based on the project you're making.

Single-Frame Corner

When a single-frame corner is called for, fold the corner-frame square in half diagonally. Lay it on the corner, butting folded edges and aligning raw edges. Stitch along the raw edges, pivoting at the corner and using a ⅛" seam allowance.

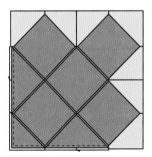

Double-Frame Corner

A double-frame corner is simply two edge frames that meet at the corner of the quilt top. Sew each edge frame into its respective seam. Finger-press and pin each frame in place. Stitch along the edges, using a ⅛" seam and pivoting at the corner.

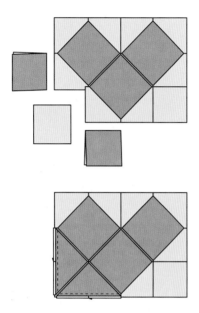

Double Edge-Diamond or Edge-Kite Frames

When two edge-diamond or edge-kite frames come together to form the corner, use the double-frame corner method. Carefully match the long edges to large foundation squares, and the short edges to small foundation squares.

Using the Blocks to Create Quilts

THE QUILTS in this book are divided into three groups. The quilt designs in each group are all based on the blocks at the beginning of each section. Just as in traditional patchwork, a number of blocks are joined together to create a quilt top. When the blocks are assembled edge to edge, all of the edge frames of the blocks that fall within the body of the quilt will match up to the edge frames of the adjoining blocks, converting the edge frames to full frames. It is also possible to use sashing between blocks, as in the "Star Sampler" quilt on page 79, so each block stands on its own.

With sashing

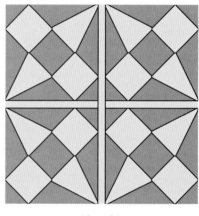

Without sashing

Joining Blocks

When joining blocks, you use the same seam construction as you did for making the individual blocks. Pin through seams at the ¼" point and stitch from pin to pin, backstitching at each end of the seam.

Pressing

Proper pressing is critical. It will determine how flat your quilt top lies. Prepare the top by making sure that all seams around the edge have been sewn all the way to the edge. You don't want any seams stopping ¼" from the outer edges.

For best results, press from the wrong side. Press seams to one side in a spiral around each intersection. Alternate the direction of the spiral from one intersection to the next. Pull the top flat as you go, and the frames will automatically be pulled into their correct position. I like to spray the seams with water as I press. Just be careful not to distort the piece if you use steam or water.

Note: *Sometimes the seams will not want to spiral. One end of a seam will want to lie one direction and the other end will want to lie in the opposite direction. When this happens, clip the seam allowances all the way to the stitching under a frame so you can press each end of the seam in the direction it wants to lie.*

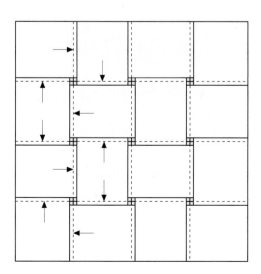

Adding Windowpanes and Borders

If you have waited to cut your windowpanes until the top is together, now is the time to decide on your fabric choices and cut them out. Cut the windowpanes from the patterns provided. They are about ¼" smaller on all sides than the frame they will fit. Use the pattern that corresponds to your frame pattern. It is not necessary to turn under any edges of the panes.

Before adding the borders, pin the edge and corner panes to their corresponding frames. The raw edge of the pane will be sewn into the border seam. Borders can either be mitered or sewn with butted (straight) edges. I have used both styles in this book.

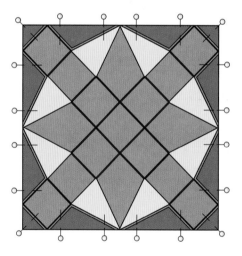

Mitered Borders

1. If there is more than one border, sew the individual border strips together lengthwise and treat them as one for this process. Finger-press a crease (or press lightly with an iron) at the center point of the top, bottom, and side border strips.

2. Lay the quilt top on a flat surface and gently smooth it out. Measure from side to side

through the center and from top to bottom through the center. Try not to stretch the foundation. Double-check to make sure your length and width measurements are correct.

3. For the side border strips, measure out from the center point exactly half the measurement of the length of the quilt. Mark this length on each end of both side borders. Measure ¼" in from each mark and make another mark. Repeat for the top and bottom borders, using the width measurement of your quilt.

4. Place a border strip, right sides together, on top of the quilt top, matching the border-strip center point with the center point of the quilt top. Match the end marks with the quilt corners. Pin in place.

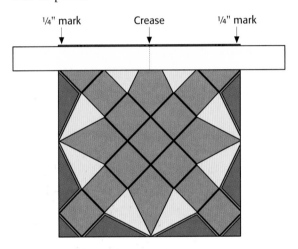

5. Using a ¼" seam, start sewing ¼" from the quilt corner, backstitch, and then sew to the other corner. Stop at the mark ¼" from the end and backstitch. Be careful to keep the seams of the foundation lying in the direction they were pressed. Check and resew if necessary. Repeat for all four borders.

6. To miter the corners, fold the quilt diagonally so that two adjacent borders lie on top of each other, matching the border edges. Line up the 45-degree line on your rotary-cutting ruler with the straight edge of the border. The edge of the ruler should line up with the ¼" mark

and extend out and away from the quilt. Using a pencil or chalk pencil, carefully mark the stitching line along the edge of the ruler.

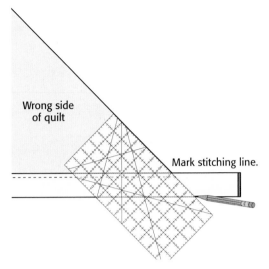

7. Pin the two borders together carefully, matching any seams and edges. Sew on the marked line, backstitching at the ¼" mark. Trim the seams to ¼". Press the seams toward the side borders. Repeat for the remaining corners.

Butted Borders

1. Lay the quilt top on a flat surface and gently smooth it out. Measure across the quilt center from top to bottom, raw edge to raw edge, being careful not to stretch the foundation. Cut two side border strips the exact length of your quilt measurement.

2. Pin the strips to the sides of the quilt top, then stitch using a ¼" seam. Sew slowly, keeping the panes lined up and making sure the seam allowances of the foundation grid lie in the direction pressed. Check the finished seams for any errant seam allowances and resew if necessary. Press the seam allowances toward the border.

3. Repeat this process for the top and bottom borders, carefully measuring across the center of the quilt from side to side, including the side borders you just added. Cut the remaining

two border strips to this exact measurement. Pin and sew, backstitching at the raw edges. Press the seams toward the border.

Finishing Your Quilt

MANY OF the steps toward finishing your Cathedral Stars quilt are just like those used for any other traditional quilt. You'll want to pay special attention to the sections on tacking the window frames and quilting your project, as these are special techniques used for these projects.

Piecing the Quilt Backing

If the measurement of your quilt back, including a few inches needed for take-up during quilting, is larger than one width of fabric, you'll need to piece a backing. When doing so, be sure to balance what you add. Instead of having a seam in the middle of the quilt, add equal amounts to the sides of one width of fabric.

Basting the Quilt

At this point, you are ready to baste the quilt layers together. Both the backing and batting should be a few inches larger all the way around than the quilt top.

1. Spread the backing on a flat surface, right side down, and tape or clip it to the surface so it won't slide or buckle. Smooth the batting over the backing, and then position the quilt top, right side up, on top of the batting. Smooth out the layers.

2. Starting in the center and working out, pin-baste with safety pins. If you are using windowpane pieces, place them on top of each frame first and then pin-baste through them. I prefer size 2 or curved safety pins. You will have to pin slightly off center to avoid the thickest areas. Use two pins in each frame on the larger frames.

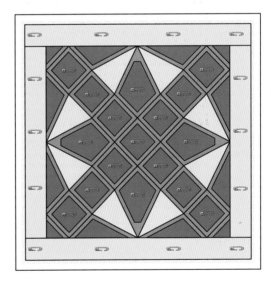

Tacking the Frames

At each corner of the window frame, you will pull back the edges of the frame to cover the corner and edges of the windowpane fabric.

Set your sewing machine for a bar tack, which is a zigzag stitch with no forward motion. It stitches back and forth, but not forward. Drop your feed dogs or cover them. Set the stitch length to 0 and your stitch width to about 2.5. Bartack at the point where the frame sides touch but do not cross, catching each side of the frame. The deeper the angle of the corner of the frame, the deeper the point at which they will cross. Move across the quilt from one corner to the next without cutting your threads. Work in one direction at a time so you don't need to turn the quilt. Do not tack the frame edges that are sewn into the borders.

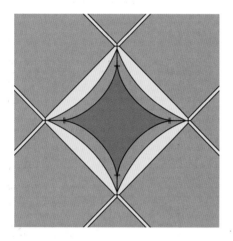

When you are finished tacking in one direction, trim the top threads first and then the back threads. Don't tug too hard or you'll pull out the threads.

Quilting Frames and Borders

After all the frame edges have been rolled back and tacked in place, it's time to stitch through the rest of the frame edges to hold them in place. Since you'll be stitching through all the layers, these stitches also serve as your quilting. You can use a straight stitch along the frame edge, or you can vary the look by using a blind hem stitch or blanket stitch. When blindstitching, sew just off the edge of the frame, catching the frame edge with the stitches that swing to the side.

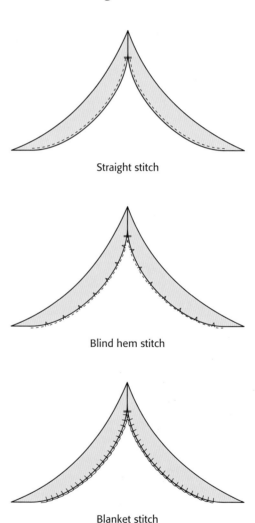

Straight stitch

Blind hem stitch

Blanket stitch

The window frames should pull back and lie flat fairly consistently. You don't need to pin them. As you sew, gently push or pull the edge toward the center of the frame. Be careful not to pull it too much or it will create a pull or pucker at the corners. Likewise, if you do not push it enough, it will create a tuck at the end of the stitching line.

Stitch from one tack to the next. I usually take just one stitch over the tack, which is normally at the center point, and, leaving the needle down, pivot. On the smaller quilts, I stitch all the way around each frame, turning the quilt as I go and backstitching at the beginning and end of each window. This technique becomes too cumbersome on large quilts, however. On those I work in rows across the quilt, backstitching at each corner. When you finish stitching in one direction, trim the threads, or they will be in the way when you quilt perpendicular rows.

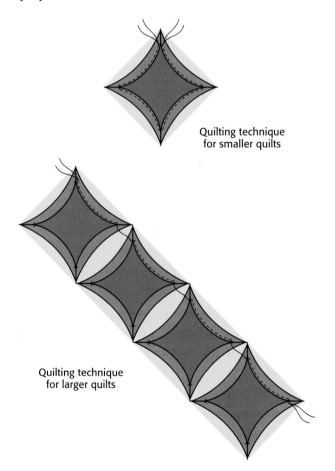

Quilting technique
for smaller quilts

Quilting technique
for larger quilts

If the quilt has borders, you can quilt right up to the borders. If there are no borders, wait until the binding is sewn on before you quilt the edge frames. When you quilt the edge frames along the borders, you will be able to start at one point and work your way all the way around the quilt without stopping to cut your threads. Remember, you don't tack these corners. You just lay the frame edges up against the border seam and stitch them down. Be careful not to lap them over the border seam, but be sure they touch the border, or the raw edges of the windowpane fabric will show.

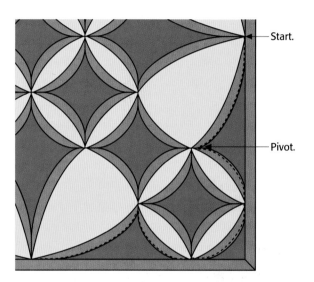

Start.

Pivot.

Quilting the Open Areas and Borders

I like to quilt in the open areas and borders by using circle templates cut from Contac paper. The sizes of the templates correspond to the finished foundation sizes: 2", 2½", 4", and 5". Draft circle templates slightly smaller to allow room for stitching. Line up the edges of the template with the points of the frames, press the templates lightly to the top of your quilt, and sew along the edge of the template from point to point, switching template sizes as needed. You can peel the templates off your quilt top and reuse them several times before they will no longer stick. When quilting the teardrop you will straighten your lines of stitching at the narrow end to meet the seam intersection. It is also possible to stipple stitch or even hand quilt these open areas.

When quilting the borders, line up two sides of the circle with three points of an edge frame. Stitch along the edge of the template, pivoting where each frame point meets the border. You should be able to quilt all the way around all four borders without breaking your thread.

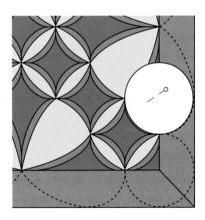

To finish your quilting, align the circle template with the center point of the previously quilted half circle and two frame points. Half of the template will be positioned off the border. Stitch around the

template, beginning and ending at the raw edge of the border.

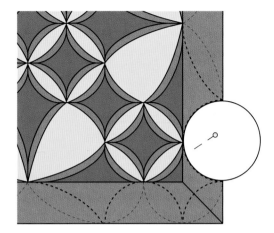

If the quilt does not have borders, you need to wait until the binding is attached before you can quilt the edge frames. Once the edges are bound, you can quilt the edge frames as described above, then hand sew the binding to the quilt back as described on the following pages.

Binding Your Quilt

Use your favorite method to cut binding strips for the quilt edges. Sometimes I cut my bindings on the bias; sometimes I don't. Some fabrics look nicer cut one way or the other, so the choice is yours.

Cutting Straight-Grain Binding

Cut 2½"-wide strips across the width of the fabric. Cut enough strips to total the circumference of the quilt plus 10".

Cutting Bias Binding

Bias binding requires more fabric than straight-grain binding. Most quilts in this book require ½ to ⅝ yard of binding fabric.

1. Straighten the raw edges of the fabric with the rotary cutter and cut off the selvage. Then fold

one short edge of the fabric diagonally so that it meets the adjacent raw edge. Lay your ruler along the fold and cut off just the very edge of the fold.

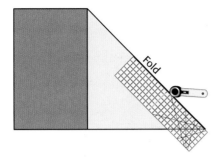

2. Set aside the triangle that you just cut off your fabric. Then cut 2½"-wide strips from the bias edge. Cut enough strips to total the circumference of the quilt plus 10".

Making and Attaching the Binding

1. Sew the strips together end to end, using diagonal seams.

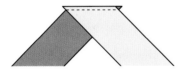

2. Press the seams flat. Fold under one end of the strip at a 90-degree angle and press. Then press the entire strip in half lengthwise.

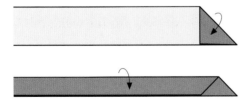

3. Trim away the excess backing fabric and batting ⅛" from the raw edge of the quilt top.

4. Place the binding on the quilt top, aligning the raw edges of the binding with the raw edges of the quilt. Sew the binding to the quilt using a ⅜" seam. A walking foot will help keep all layers feeding evenly through your machine.

5. As you approach the corner, measure ⅜" in from the adjacent edge of the quilt and mark the distance with a pin. Stitch to the pin, and with the needle down, raise the presser foot and turn the corner of the top toward you. Stitch off the corner at a diagonal.

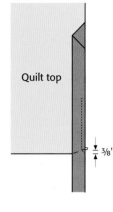

Quilt top

⅜"

6. Fold the binding up at a 90-degree angle to form a 45-degree fold in the binding.

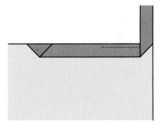

7. Fold the binding back onto itself, so the fold aligns with the raw edge of the quilt top.

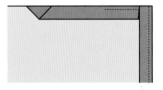

8. Begin stitching at the raw edge. Stitch to the next corner, repeating the stopping and folding process for the corner. Repeat for all corners.

9. To complete the binding, stitch the end of the binding on top of the folded beginning section. Slightly angle this end so it is narrower than the beginning section and will easily slip inside the beginning fold.

10. If you have edge frames that need to be quilted, do so now. Then fold the binding to the back of the quilt, folding a miter into each corner, and slipstitch into place.

PART TWO

Floating the Windows, Creating Stars

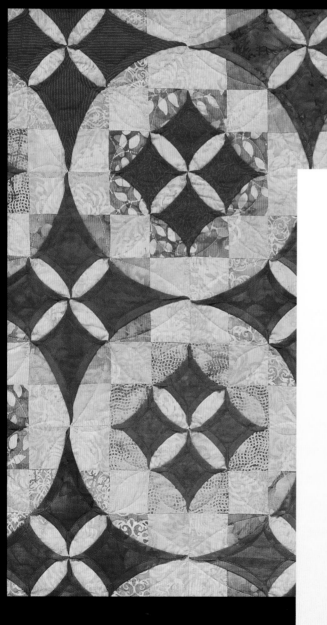

The blocks in this chapter are simple, four-frame designs. Floating Window is a basic four-square frame block and a perfect starting point. Floating Star is a four-pointed star design made with kite-shaped frames. If you split the Floating Star block vertically and horizontally and rotate its sections to the outside, you get the Split Floating Star block. The Floating Window/Star Combination block is just what its name implies, a combination of the first two blocks.

THE BLOCKS

FLOATING WINDOW

FLOATING STAR

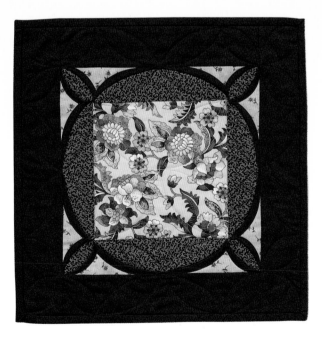

SPLIT FLOATING STAR

FLOATING WINDOW/STAR COMBINATION

Floating Window

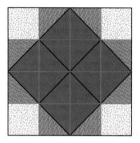

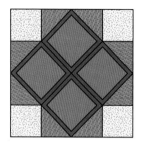

Foundation and Frame Grid

Pane Layout

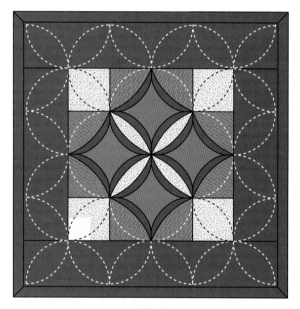

8" block

Block Assembly

1. Construct a 4-frame unit using 4 light print 2½" foundation squares for the center and 8 medium stripe 2½" foundation squares for the top, bottom, and 2 sides. Refer to "Sewing Square Frames" on page 9.

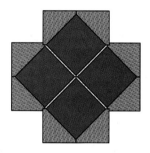

2. Use the 4 remaining 2½" light print foundation squares for the corners. Refer to "Joining Blocks" on page 15 to assemble the block.

3. To turn your block into a small wall hanging, cut 3"-wide strips for borders. Refer to "Butted Borders" on page 16. See "Finishing Your Quilt" on page 17 for directions on adding the windowpanes, quilting, and binding.

Cutting

Pieces	Fabric	First Cut	Second Cut
Foundations	Light print	1 strip, 2½" x 42"	8 squares, 2½" x 2½"
	Medium stripe	1 strip, 2½" x 42"	8 squares, 2½" x 2½"
Frames	Dark olive	1 strip, 4½" x 42"	4 squares, 4½" x 4½"
Panes	Fuchsia	1 strip, 2" x 42"	4 squares, 2" x 2"

Floating Star

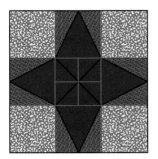

Foundation and Frame Grid

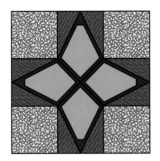

Pane Layout

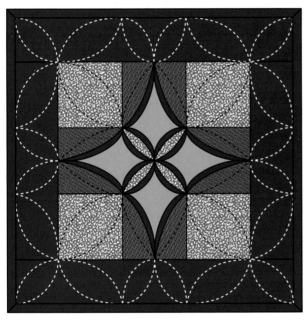

12" block

Block Assembly

1. Construct a star unit using 4 dark print template A kite frames. Refer to "Sewing Kite Frames Using Foundation Rectangles" on page 11.

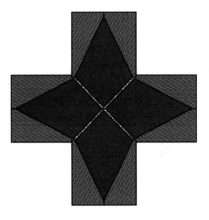

2. Add the 4½" light print corner squares to complete the block, referring to "Joining Blocks" on page 15.

3. To turn your block into a small wall hanging, cut 3"-wide strips for borders. Refer to "Butted Borders" on page 16. See "Finishing Your Quilt" on page 17 for directions on adding the windowpanes, quilting, and binding.

Cutting

Pieces	Fabric	First Cut	Second Cut
Foundations	Light print	1 strip, 2½" x 42"	4 squares, 2½" x 2½"
		1 strip, 4½" x 42"	4 squares, 4½" x 4½"
	Medium stripe	1 strip, 2½" x 42"	8 rectangles, 2½" x 4½"
Frames	Dark print	1 strip, 7⅛" x 42"	4 template A
Panes	Medium solid	1 strip, 3¼" x 42"	4 template A-WP

Split Floating Star

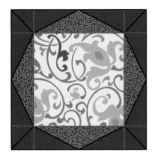

Foundation and Frame Grid

Pane Layout

12" block

Block Assembly

1. On the wrong side of the 8½" yellow floral foundation square, mark ¼" from each corner. To each side of the square, sew 1 medium blue 2½" x 8½" foundation rectangle, sewing from mark to mark and backstitching at each end.

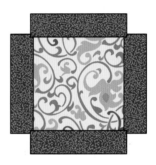

2. Add 2 dark blue template C edge-kite frames to each corner, using a medium blue 2½" foundation square for each. Refer to "Double Edge-Diamond or Edge-Kite Frames" on page 14.

3. To turn your block into a small wall hanging, cut 3"-wide strips for borders. Refer to "Butted Borders" on page 16. See "Finishing Your Quilt" on page 17 for directions on adding the windowpanes, quilting, and binding.

Cutting

Pieces	Fabric	First Cut	Second Cut
Foundations	Yellow floral	1 square, 8½" x 8½"	
	Medium blue print	2 strips, 2½" x 42"	4 squares, 2½" x 2½"
			4 rectangles, 2½" x 8½"
Frames	Dark blue solid	1 strip, 4" x 42"	8 template C
Panes	Yellow print	1 strip, 2" x 42"	8 template C-WP

Floating Window/Star Combination

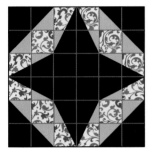

Foundation and Frame Grid

Pane Layout

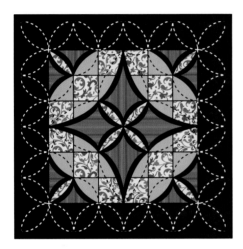

12" block

Block Assembly

1. Sew a multicolor print 2½" foundation square to a light green batik 2½" foundation square. Repeat to make 8 pairs.

Make 8.

2. Construct the star unit by sewing the first seam of 4 dark purple template A kite frames to the multicolor print squares. Complete each kite frame by sewing the long sides of the kites to the sewn pairs of multicolor print and light

Cutting

Pieces	Fabric	First Cut	Second Cut
Foundations	Multicolor print	2 strips, 2½" x 42"	20 squares, 2½" x 2½"
	Light green batik	1 strip, 2½" x 42"	16 squares, 2½" x 2½"
Frames	Dark purple	1 strip, 7⅛" x 42"	4 template A
		1 strip, 2½" x 42"	8 rectangles, 2½" x 4½"
Panes	Blue stripe	1 strip, 3¼" x 42"	4 template A-WP
		1 strip, 2½" x 12"	4 squares, 2½" x 2½", cut in half diagonally

green batik squares. Be sure to orient the squares so the multicolor print is at the outer edges of the block. Set aside.

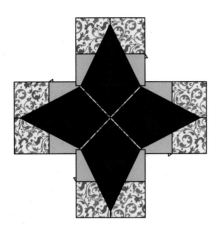

3. Construct 4 corner units by sewing 2 multicolor print and 2 light green batik 2½" foundation squares together. Add a dark purple 2½" x 4½" rectangular edge frame to 2 sides of a multicolor print 2½" foundation square. Refer to "Double-Frame Corner" on page 14.

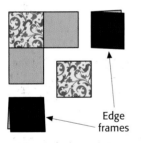

Edge
frames

4. Sew each of the corner units into the blocks, with the edge frames toward the outside. Refer to "Joining Blocks" on page 15 for details.

5. To turn your block into a small wall hanging, cut 3"-wide strips for borders. Refer to "Butted Borders" on page 16. See "Finishing Your Quilt" on page 17 for quilting and binding directions.

Floating Windows

Shelley Swanland, 2000, Cayucos, California, 40" x 50".
The most basic of Cathedral Window blocks creates an intricate pattern
reminiscent of beautiful Middle Eastern mosaic designs.

Quilt Plan

Quilt Size: 40" x 50"
10" Floating Window block: Make 20.

Materials

	Fabric	Amount
Foundations	Dark blue print	1⅛ yds.
	Dark blue polka dot	1⅛ yds.
Frames	Light blue print	1⅞ yds.
Panes	Blue star print	⅜ yd.
Backing and binding		3¼ yds.
Batting		46" x 56"

Cutting *Cut all pieces in the order listed below.*

Pieces	Fabric	First Cut	Second Cut
Foundations	Dark blue print	13 strips, 3" x 42"	160 squares, 3" x 3"
	Dark blue polka dot	13 strips, 3" x 42"	160 squares, 3" x 3"
Frames	Light blue print	12 strips, 5½" x 42"	80 squares, 5½" x 5½"
Panes	Blue star print	6 strips, 2½" x 42"	80 squares, 2½" x 2½"

Quilt Top Assembly

1. Following the instructions for the Floating Window block on page 24, make a total of 20 blocks. Make 10 blocks using the dark blue print for the 4 inner foundation squares, the dark blue polka dot for the foundation sides, and the dark blue print to finish the foundation corners. For the remaining 10 blocks, swap the placement of the dark blue print and dark blue polka dot fabrics.

 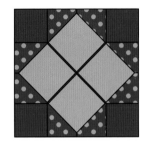

2. Lay out the blocks for the quilt top in rows, alternating the 2 block variations. You'll have 5 rows of 4 blocks each. Sew the blocks into rows, referring to "Joining Blocks" on page 15.

3. Press the quilt top, referring to "Pressing" on page 15.

4. Piece the quilt backing. It should measure approximately 46" x 56". Layer the backing, batting, and quilt top. Lay out the windowpane squares, placing one in the center of each frame. Pin-baste through the center of each frame and through each corner of each block, starting at the center and working outward. Machine tack the frames in place, then quilt the window frames and the exposed foundation areas.

5. Refer to "Finishing Your Quilt" on page 17 for making and attaching the binding. You will need a 2½"-wide binding strip at least 190" long.

Checkerboard Stars

Shelley Swanland, 2000, Cayucos, California 44" x 44".
The simple Four Patch is elevated to new heights with the
addition of bold and dramatic four-pointed Cathedral Stars.

Quilt Plan

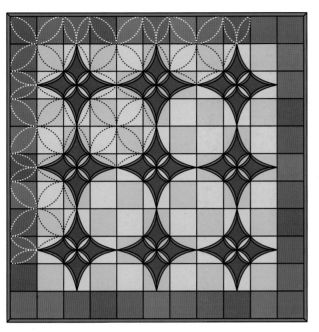

Quilt Size: 44" x 44"
12" Floating Star block: Make 9.

Materials

	Fabric	Amount
Foundations	Medium print	¾ yd.
	Light print	⅞ yd.
Frames and borders	5 assorted purple prints	⅝ yd. *each*
Panes	2 dark purple prints	¼ yd. *each*
Backing and binding		2⅞ yds.
Batting		50" x 50"

Cutting   *Cut all pieces in the order listed below.*

Pieces	Fabric	First Cut	Second Cut
Foundations	Medium print	3 strips, 4½" x 42"	20 squares, 4½" x 4½"
		1 strip, 2½" x 42"	16 squares, 2½" x 2½"
		2 strips, 4½" x 42"	32 rectangles, 2½" x 4½"
	Light print	2 strips, 4½" x 42"	16 squares, 4½" x 4½"
		2 strips, 2½" x 42"	20 squares, 2½" x 2½"
		3 strips, 4½" x 42"	40 rectangles, 2½" x 4½"
Frames	Purple prints (5)	9 strips, 7⅛" x 42"	36 template A, 4 from each strip
Panes	Dark purple print 1	2 strips, 3¼" x 42"	16 template A-WP
	Dark purple print 2	2 strips, 3¼" x 42"	20 template A-WP
Borders	Purple prints (5)	1 strip of each, 4½" x 42"	40 squares, 4½" x 4½"

Quilt Top Assembly

1. Following the instructions for the Floating Star block on page 25, use the light print 2½" x 4½" foundation rectangles and 2½" foundation squares to make 5 blocks. Use the medium print 4½" foundation squares for the corners. Then make 4 blocks, reversing the fabric placement. You will have 4 blocks with light corners and 5 blocks with dark corners.

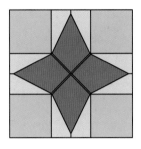 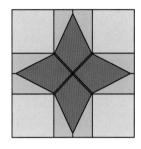

2. Lay out the blocks for the top in rows, alternating the 2 block variations. Sew the blocks together, referring to "Joining Blocks" on page 15. Sew the seams around the edge of the quilt top all the way to the edge.

3. Press the quilt top, referring to "Pressing" on page 15.

4. Referring to the quilt plan, sew the 40 purple 4½" border squares into strips. Sew the strips to the top carefully, so that seams lie in the direction they were pressed.

5. Piece the quilt backing. It should measure approximately 50" x 50". Layer the backing, batting, and quilt top. Lay out the windowpane squares, placing one in the center of each frame. Pin-baste in the center of each frame and through each corner foundation square, starting at the center and working outward. Machine tack the frames in place, then quilt the frames and exposed areas of the foundation.

6. Refer to "Finishing Your Quilt" on page 17 for making and attaching the binding. You will need a 2½"-wide binding strip at least 186" long.

Stars All Around

Shelley Swanland, 2000, Cayucos, California, 47" x 58".

The Split Floating Star block offers plenty of opportunity to showcase a favorite fabric, such as the bright and cheery 1940s print shown here. The stars form a lattice while the theme fabric shines.

Quilt Plan

Quilt Side: 47" x 58"
12" Split Floating Star block: Make 20.

Materials

	Fabric	Amount
Foundations and panes	Multicolor print 1	1¼ yds.
	Multicolor print 2	¾ yd.
	Blue print	1¾ yds.
Frames	Red solid	2⅜ yds.
Backing		3⅝ yds.
Binding	Red solid	½ yd.
Batting		53" x 64"

Cutting *Cut all pieces in the order listed below.*

Pieces	Fabric	First Cut	Second Cut
Foundations	Multicolor print 1	5 strips, 8½" x 42"	20 squares, 8½" x 8½"
	Blue print	5 strips, 2½" x 42"	80 squares, 2½" x 2½"
		5 strips, 8½" x 42"	80 rectangles, 2½" x 8½"
Frames	Red solid	9 strips, 7⅛" x 42"	62 template A
		4 strips, 4" x 42"	18 template C
			18 template C reversed
Panes	Multicolor print 2	5 strips, 3¼" x 42"	62 template A-WP
		4 strips, 2" x 42"	18 template C-WP
			18 template C-WP reversed

Quilt Top Assembly

1. On the wrong side of the 8½" multicolor print foundation squares, mark ¼" from each corner. To each side of these squares, sew 1 blue print 2½" x 8½" foundation rectangle, sewing from mark to mark and backstitching at each end. Make 20 of these center units.

2. Assemble 4 rows of 5 blocks each as follows: place 2 red template A kite frames, folded in half lengthwise, between 2 blue print rectangle sides of 2 center units. Refer to "Kite Frames" on page 11 for detailed instructions.

3. Complete the 2 kite frames, adding 2 blue print 2½" foundation squares to each. Continue adding kite frames and center units until you have 5 center units connected with 4 sets of kite frames.

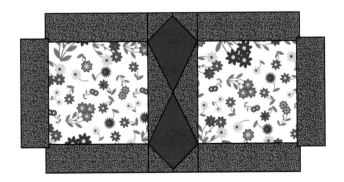

4. Repeat steps 2 and 3 three more times so you have 4 rows of 5 blocks each.

5. Connect the rows by adding 2 kite frames between each pair of 2 center units. Complete each kite frame. The 2½" blue print squares are already attached to the adjacent kite frames; the 2½" blue print squares will only be added at the top and bottom of each row.

6. Add the red template C edge-kite frames to the outer edge, adding a 2½" blue print foundation square at each corner.

7. From the wrong side, press the kite frames first, spiraling the seams at the center of each star. Once the seams are flat, press the seams of the 8½" squares toward the sashing, folding back 1 seam allowance at each corner.

8. Piece the quilt backing so it measures approximately 53" x 64". Layer the backing, batting, and quilt top. Lay out the windowpane squares, placing one in the center of each frame. Pin-baste through the center of each pane and add several more pins through each block, starting at the quilt center and working outward. Machine quilt the frames in place, then quilt all of the frames except the edge frames. Using an 8" freezer-paper circle template, quilt the blocks as shown.

9. See "Finishing Your Quilt" on page 17 for making and attaching the binding. You will need a 2½"-wide binding strip at least 220" long.

Stars on Fire

Shelley Swanland, 2000, Cayucos, California, 43½" x 56½".
You can really spice things up when you set together rows of seemingly simple Floating Window/Star combinations. Notice how a secondary pattern emerges—and with no extra work! If you prefer to turn down the heat, substitute cool blues, purples, and green for an icy version of this sizzling design.

Quilt Plan

Quilt Size: 43½" x 56½"
12" Floating Window/Star combination: Make 12.

Materials

	Fabric	Amount
Foundations	Light yellow print	1⅛ yds.
	Assorted medium prints	1 yd. *total*
Frames and borders	Assorted orange and red prints	3¼ yds. *total*
Backing		3 yds.
Binding	Red print	⅝ yd.
Batting		50" x 63"

Cutting   *Cut all pieces in the order listed below.*

Pieces	Fabric	First Cut	Second Cut
Foundations	Light yellow print	15 strips, 2½" x 42"	240 squares, 2½" x 2½"
	Medium prints	12 strips, 2½" x 42"	192 squares, 2½" x 2½"
Frames	Assorted orange and red prints	7 strips, 7⅛" x 42"	48 template A
		5 strips, 4½" x 42"	34 squares, 4½" x 4½"
		2 strips, 4½" x 42"	28 rectangles, 2½" x 4½"
Borders	Orange and red prints	6 strips, 4½" x 42"	46 squares, 4½" x 4½"

Note: This quilt does not contain windowpane pieces.

Quilt Top Assembly

1. Using 96 light yellow 2½" foundation squares and 96 medium print 2½" foundation squares in groups of 8 matching fabrics, sew the squares together in sets of 2.

2. Construct 12 star units, using 12 sets of 4 orange/red template A kite frames and the 2-patch units made in step 1. Position the foundation pieces or units so the light yellow squares are toward the outside. Use light yellow 2½" foundation squares for the centers.

3. Construct 6 square units, using 6 sets of 4 orange/red 4½" square frames, 8 medium print 2½" foundation squares, and 8 light yellow 2½" foundation squares. Use the light yellow squares in the center and outer corners.

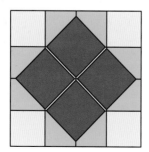

4. Make 10 side units, using 2 orange/red 2½" x 4½" rectangular frames, 1 orange/red 4½" square frame, 4 medium print 2½" foundation squares, and 4 light yellow 2½" foundation squares for each. Use the light yellow squares for the center and corners.

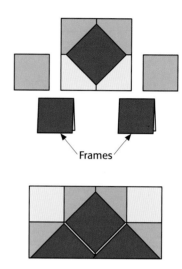

Frames

5. Make 4 corner units, using 2 orange/red 2½" x 4½" rectangular frames and 2 each of medium print and light yellow 2½" foundation squares.

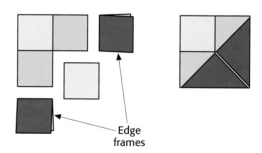

Edge frames

6. Lay out 12 star units, 5 square units, 10 side units, and 4 corner units, following the quilt plan. Sew the units together, using the same seam method used for block construction and referring to "Joining Blocks" on page 15. Sew the seams around the edge of the quilt top all the way to the edge.

7. Press the quilt top, referring to "Pressing" on page 15. Clip the long seam allowances of the

stars to make the seams lie flat. Clip to the stitching behind the frames.

8. Referring to the quilt plan, lay out the 46 orange/red 4½" border squares. Sew the squares into strips. Sew the strips to the top carefully, so that seams lie in the direction they were pressed.

9. Piece the quilt backing so it measures approximately 50" x 63". Layer the backing, batting, and quilt top. Pin-baste through the center of each frame and through each corner founda-tion square, starting at the quilt center and working outward.

10. Machine tack the frames, then quilt the window frames and the exposed foundation areas. Quilt the border last, referring to the quilt plan on page 39.

11. Refer to "Finishing Your Quilt" on page 17 for making and attaching the binding. You will need a 2½"-wide binding strip at least 190" long.

PART THREE

Expanding the Stars, Adding Windows

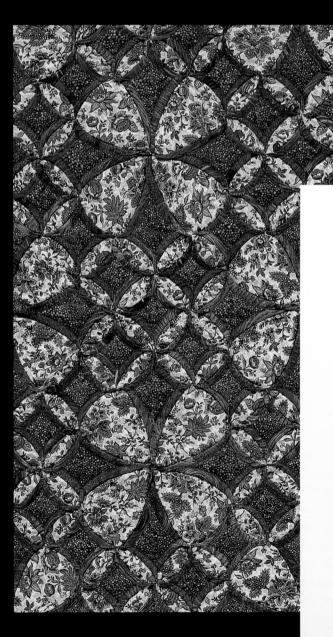

The blocks in this section have more components than the Floating Window and Floating Star blocks and variations in Part Two. While they look complex, the stitching techniques used to make these blocks are the same, and they use squares in only two sizes for their foundations.

THE BLOCKS

CATHEDRAL STAR

SPLIT CATHEDRAL STAR

MORNING STAR

SPLIT MORNING STAR

Cathedral Star

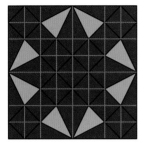

Foundation and Frame Grid

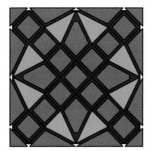

Pane Layout

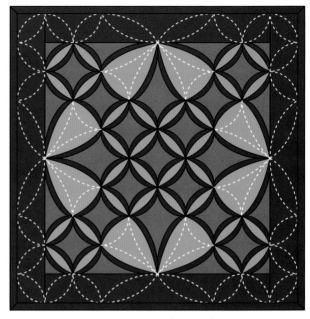

16" block

Cutting

Pieces	Fabric	First Cut	Second Cut
Foundations	Blue print	2 strips, 2½" x 42"	32 squares, 2½" x 2½"
		1 strip, 4½" x 42"	8 squares, 4½" x 4½"
Frames	Dark green print	1 strip, 7⅛" x 42"	4 template A
		1 strip, 4" x 42"	4 template C
			4 template C reversed
		2 strips, 4½" x 42"	13 squares, 4½" x 4½"
		1 strip, 2½" x 42"	4 squares, 2½" x 2½"
Panes	Medium green print	1 strip, 3¼" x 42"	4 template A-WP
		1 strip, 2" x 42"	4 template C-WP
			4 template C-WP reversed
		1 strip, 2" x 42"	15 squares, 2" x 2"; cut 2 squares in half diagonally

Block Assembly

1. Construct a single square frame, using 4 blue print 2½" foundation squares and 1 dark green 4½" square frame.

2. Add another 4½" square frame to each corner of the first square, creating a 5-frame center. Refer to "Sewing Square Frames" on page 9 for details.

3. Add 4 dark green template A kite frames one at a time, working around the center. Sew the short end of the kite frame between the 2 foundation squares. Sew 2 blue 4½" foundation squares to the long edges of the kite frame. Sew the 2 remaining seams, using only half of the larger foundation square.

4. At each corner, 1 small foundation square and the remaining half of 2 large foundation squares come together. Add a dark green 4½" square frame at this point. You will need to add 1 more small foundation square.

5. Add another dark green 4½" square frame to each corner.

6. Add 8 dark green template C edge-kite frames and 4 dark green 2½" square frames to complete the block.

7. To turn your block into a wall hanging, cut 3"-wide strips for borders. Refer to "Butted Borders" on page 16. See "Finishing Your Quilt" on page 17 to add the windowpanes and complete your project.

Split Cathedral Star

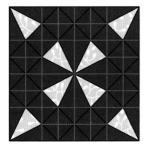

Foundation and Frame Grid

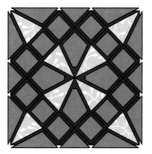

Pane Layout

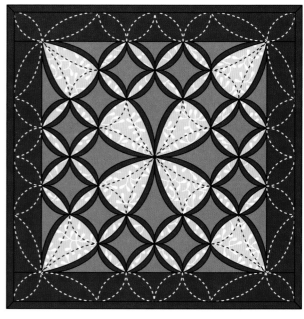

16" block

Cutting

Pieces	Fabric	First Cut	Second Cut
Foundations	Light pink print	2 strips, 2½" x 42"	32 squares, 2½" x 2½"
		1 strip, 4½" x 42"	8 squares, 4½" x 4½"
Frames	Dark red	1 strip, 7⅛" x 42"	4 template A
		1 strip, 4" x 42"	4 template C
			4 template C reversed
		2 strips, 4½" x 42"	12 squares, 4½" x 4½"
			4 rectangles, 2½" x 4½"
Panes	Medium red	1 strip, 3¼" x 42"	4 template A-WP
		1 strip, 2" x 42"	4 template C-WP
			4 template C-WP reversed
		1 strip, 2" x 42"	12 squares, 2" x 2"
		2 squares, 2½" x 2½"	4 triangles; cut squares in half diagonally

Block Assembly

1. Sew the long seam of 4 dark red template A kite frames and 4 light pink 4½" foundation squares, referring to "Sewing Diamond and Kite Frames Using Large Foundation Squares" on page 12.

2. Sew the seam on the opposite end of each kite frame, adding 2 light pink 2½" foundation squares. Sew the remaining seams. Each seam should use only half of the large foundation squares as described on page 12.

3. At each corner, 2 small foundation squares and the remaining half of 1 large foundation square come together. Add a dark red 4½" square frame at this point. You will need to add 1 more large foundation square to each.

4. Add 8 dark red 4½" square frames, placing 2 on each side of the block center.

5. Add 4 dark red 2½" x 4½" rectangular edge frames, one in the center of each side.

6. Add 8 dark red template C edge-kite frames to complete the block.

7. To turn your block into a wall hanging, cut 3"-wide strips for borders. Refer to "Butted Borders" on page 16. See "Finishing Your Quilt" on page 17 to add the windowpanes and complete your project.

Morning Star

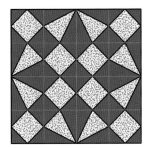

Foundation and Frame Grid

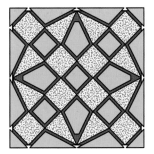

Pane Layout

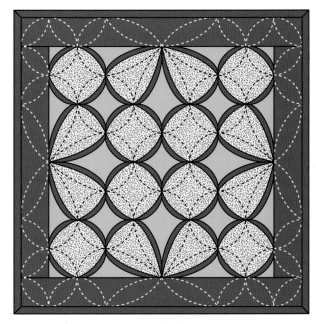

16" block

Cutting

Pieces	Fabric	First Cut	Second Cut
Foundations	Shell print	2 strips, 4½" x 42"	16 squares, 4½" x 4½"
Frames	Dark rust	1 strip, 7⅛" x 42"	4 template A
		1 strip, 4" x 42"	4 template C
			4 template C reversed
		1 strip, 4½" x 42"	5 squares, 4½" x 4½"
		1 strip, 2½" x 12"	4 squares, 2½" x 2½"
Panes	Peach	1 strip, 3¼" x 42"	4 template A-WP
		1 strip, 2" x 42"	4 template C-WP
			4 template C-WP reversed
		1 strip, 2" x 42"	5 squares, 2" x 2"
		2 squares, 2½" x 2½"	4 triangles; cut squares in half diagonally

Block Assembly

This block uses only large foundation squares. Refer to "Sewing Diamond and Kite Frames Using Large Foundation Squares" on page 12.

1. Sew the short end of 4 dark rust template A kite frames, tails pointing outward, around 1 dark rust 4½" square frame, using 4 shell print 4½" foundation squares.

2. Sew the opposite end of each kite frame, using 2 shell print 4½" foundation squares for each.

3. As you complete the remaining seams of the kite frames, add a dark rust 4½" square frame in each corner. You will need another foundation square to complete each frame.

4. Add 8 dark rust template C edge-kite frames and 4 dark rust 2½" square frames to the block.

5. To turn your block into a wall hanging, cut 3"-wide strips for borders. Refer to "Butted Borders" on page 16. See "Finishing Your Quilt" on page 17 to add the windowpanes and complete your project.

Split Morning Star

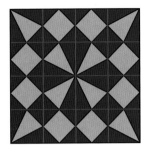

Foundation and Frame Grid

Pane Layout

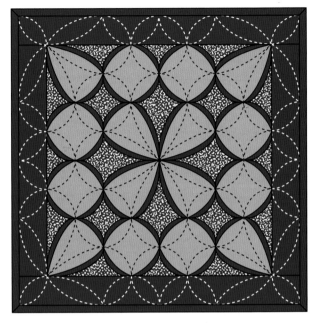

16" block

Cutting

Pieces	Fabric	First Cut	Second Cut
Foundations	Light blue print	2 strips, 4½" x 42"	16 squares, 4½" x 4½"
Frames	Dark blue solid	1 strip, 7⅛" x 42"	4 template A
		1 strip, 4" x 42"	4 template C
			4 template C reversed
		1 strip, 4½" x 42"	4 squares, 4½" x 4½"
			4 rectangles, 2½" x 4½"
Panes	Dark blue print	1 strip, 3¼" x 42"	4 template A-WP
			2 squares, 2½" x 2½"; cut in half diagonally
		1 strip, 2" x 42"	4 template C-WP
			4 template C-WP reversed
		1 strip, 2" x 42"	4 squares, 2" x 2"

Block Assembly

This block uses only large foundation squares. Refer to "Sewing Diamond and Kite Frames Using Large Foundation Squares" on page 12 for detailed instructions.

1. Sew the long end of 4 template A kite frames together, using 4 light blue 4½" foundation squares. Tails should face toward the center of the block.

2. Sew the opposite end of each kite frame, adding 2 light blue 4½" foundation squares and 1 dark blue 2½" x 4½" rectangular edge frame in each seam.

3. As you complete the remaining seams of the kite frames, add a dark blue 4½" square frame in each corner. You will need to add another foundation square.

4. Add 8 dark blue template C edge-kite frames to the edges of the block. Tails should be pointing toward the block corners.

5. To turn your block into a wall hanging, cut 3"-wide strips for borders. Refer to "Butted Borders" on page 16. See "Finishing Your Quilt" on page 17 to add the windowpanes and complete your project.

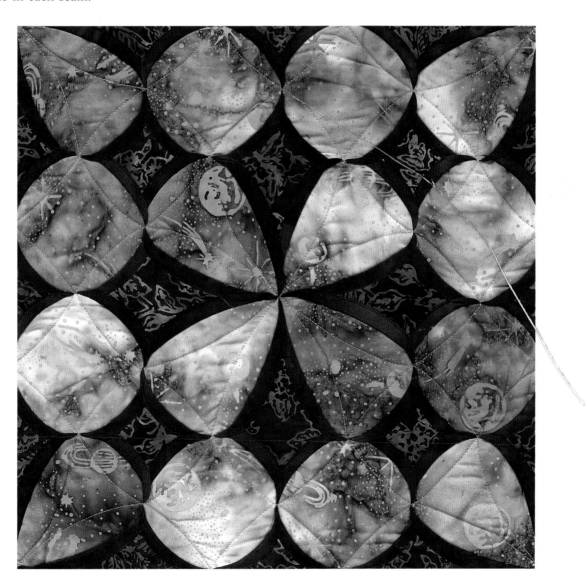

Shells, Stars, and Stone

Shelley Swanland, 2000, Cayucos, California, 50" x 50".
Turn the Cathedral Star block into a graphic statement by using high-contrast
colors in your quilt. Set on a pale foundation, the stars really pop, while a secondary
pattern of large, interlocking circles adds movement to the design.

Quilt Plan

Quilt Size: 50" x 50"
20" Cathedral Star block: Make 4.

Materials

	Fabric	Amount
Foundations	Light multicolor batik	2 yds.
Frames	Dark navy blue	3½ yds.
Panes	Shell batik	½ yd.
	Star batik	⅛ yd.
	Stone-print batik	½ yd.
Borders and binding	Dark navy blue	1⅝ yds.
Backing		3⅜ yds.
Batting		56" x 56"

Cutting *Cut all pieces in the order listed below.*

Pieces	Fabric	First Cut	Second Cut
Foundations	Light multicolor batik	11 strips, 3" x 42"	128 squares, 3" x 3"
		5 strips, 5½" x 42"	32 squares, 5½" x 5½"
Frames	Dark navy blue	6 strips, 8" x 42"	24 template E
		8 strips, 5½" x 42"	53 squares, 5½" x 5½"
		4 strips, 4¾" x 42"	8 template G
			8 template G reversed
		1 strip, 3" x 42"	4 rectangles, 3" x 5½"
			4 squares, 3" x 3"
Panes	Shell batik	2 strips, 4" x 42"	16 template E-WP
		2 strips, 2½" x 42"	20 squares, 2½" x 2½"
	Star batik	1 strip, 2½" x 42"	16 squares, 2½" x 2½"
	Stone-print batik	1 strip, 4" x 42"	8 template E-WP
		2 strips, 2½" x 42"	19 squares, 2½" x 2½"; cut 2 squares in half diagonally for corners
		1 strip, 2¼" x 42"	16 template G-WP
		1 strip, 3" x 8"	2 squares, 3" x 3"; cut in half diagonally for sides
Borders	Dark navy blue	4 strips, 5½" wide, cut lengthwise	

Quilt Top Assembly

1. Following the instructions for the Cathedral Star block on page 44, make 4 blocks without adding the edge or corner frames.

2. Lay out the 4 blocks. Where each block meets another block, construct 2 kite frames. You'll need a total of 8 kite frames. In the center of the quilt where the 4 blocks meet, add 1 dark navy blue 5½" square frame.

3. Add 4 dark navy blue template G edge-kite frames to each side of the quilt (16 total). Add 1 dark navy blue 3" x 5½" rectangular frame at the center of each side of the quilt top. Add 1 dark navy blue 3" square frame to each corner.

4. Press the quilt top, referring to "Pressing" on page 15.

5. Pin the edge, side, and corner windowpanes in position, then attach the borders, referring to "Mitered Borders" on page 15 for directions.

6. Piece the quilt backing so it measures approximately 56" x 56". Layer the batting, backing, and quilt top. Lay out the windowpane squares and pin-baste through each pane and foundation, starting at the center of the quilt and working outward.

7. Machine tack the frames in place, then quilt the frames and the exposed foundation areas. Quilt the borders last.

8. See "Finishing Your Quilt" on page 17 for making and attaching the binding. You will need a 2½"-wide binding strip at least 190" long.

Interlocking Stars

Shelley Swanland, 2000, Cayucos, California, 42" x 42".

Pretty blue windowpanes seem to sparkle like jewels when surrounded by purple frames.
Similar to the "Shells, Stars, and Stone" quilt on page 52, this quilt uses the Split Cathedral Star block
rather than the basic Cathedral Star block to create four large circles that glitter with star centers.

Quilt Plan

Quilt Size: 42" x 42"
16" Split Cathedral Star block: Make 4.

Materials

	Fabric	Amount
Foundations	Light print	1¼ yds.
Frames	Purple print	2¼ yds.
Panes	Blue print	¾ yd.
Inner border	Light print	¼ yd.
Outer border and binding	Purple print	1⅜ yds.
Backing		2⅞ yds.
Batting		48" x 48"

Cutting *Cut all pieces in the order listed below.*

Pieces	Fabric	First Cut	Second Cut
Foundations	Light print	8 strips, 2½" x 42"	128 squares, 2½" x 2½"
		4 strips, 4½" x 42"	32 squares, 4½" x 4½"
Frames	Purple print	7 strips, 4½" x 42"	52 squares, 4½" x 4½"
		4 strips, 7⅛" x 42"	24 template A
		2 strips, 4" x 42"	8 template C
			8 template C reversed
		1 strip, 4½" x 42"	8 rectangles, 2½" x 4½"
Panes	Blue print	3 strips, 2" x 42"	52 squares, 2" x 2"
		2 strips, 3½" x 42"	24 template A-WP
		2 strips, 2" x 42"	8 template C-WP
			8 template C-WP reversed
		1 strip, 2½" x 12"	4 squares, 2½" x 2½"; cut in half diagonally
Inner border	Light print	4 strips, 2¼" x 42"	
Outer border	Purple print	4 strips, 4¼" x 42"	

Quilt Top Assembly

1. Following the instructions for the Split Cathedral Star block on page 46, make 4 blocks without adding the edge frames.

2. Lay out the 4 blocks. Where each block meets another block, construct 2 kite frames and 1 square frame. You'll need a total of 8 kite frames and 4 square frames.

3. Add 4 purple template C edge-kite frames to each side of the quilt (16 total). Add 2 purple 2½" x 4½" rectangular frames to each side of the quilt top (8 total).

4. Press the quilt top, referring to "Pressing" on page 15.

5. Pin the edge and side windowpanes in position, then attach the borders, referring to "Butted Borders" on page 16.

6. Piece the quilt backing so it measures approximately 48" x 48". Layer the batting, backing, and quilt top. Lay out the windowpane squares. Pin-baste through each pane and foundation, through all layers, starting at the center of the quilt and working outward.

7. Machine tack the frames in place, then quilt the frames and the exposed foundation areas. Quilt the borders last.

8. See "Finishing Your Quilt" on page 17 for making and attaching the binding. You will need a 2½"-wide binding strip at least 190" long.

Midnight Glow

Shelley Swanland, 2000, Cayucos, California, 47" x 63½".
Who wouldn't enjoy snuggling under this beautiful lap-size quilt?
Even on the cloudiest of days the stars will be shining on this gem!

Quilt Plan

Quilt Size: 47 x 63½"
16" Split Morning Star block: Make 12.

Materials

	Fabric	Amount
Foundations	Navy celestial batik	3 yds.
Frames	Fuchsia batik	3½ yds.
	Turquoise batik	1½ yds.
Panes	Light multicolor batik	1 yd.
	Turquoise print batik	⅜ yd.
Binding	Turquoise check batik	⅝ yd.
Backing		4 yds.
Batting		53" x 70"

Cutting *Cut all pieces in the order listed below.*

Pieces	Fabric	First Cut	Second Cut
Foundations	Navy celestial batik	22 strips, 4½" x 42"	192 squares, 4½" x 4½"
Frames	Fuchsia batik	4 strips, 7⅛" x 42"	82 template A
		4 strips, 4" x 42"	14 template C
			14 template C reversed
	Turquoise batik	9 strips, 4½" x 42"	65 squares, 4½" x 4½"
		1 strip, 4½" x 42"	14 rectangles, 2½" x 4½"
Panes	Light multicolor batik	6 strips, 3¼" x 42"	82 template A-WP
		3 strips, 2" x 42"	14 template C-WP
			14 template C-WP reversed
	Turquoise print batik	4 strips, 2" x 42"	65 squares, 2"x 2"
		1 strip, 2½" x 22"	7 squares, 2½" x 2½"; cut in half diagonally

Quilt Top Assembly

1. Following the instructions for the Split Morning Star block on page 50, make 12 blocks without adding the edge frames.

2. Lay out the 12 blocks. Where each block meets another block, construct 2 kite frames and 1 square frame, for a total of 34 kite frames and 17 square frames.

3. Add 8 fuchsia template C edge-kite frames to each side of the quilt top and 6 to the top and bottom edges. Add 4 turquoise 2½" x 4½" rectangular frames to each side and 3 to each of the top and bottom edges of the quilt top.

4. Press the quilt top, referring to "Pressing" on page 15.

5. Piece the quilt backing so it measures approximately 53" x 70". Layer the batting, backing, and quilt top. Lay out the windowpanes and pin-baste through each pane and foundation area, starting at the center of the quilt and working outward.

6. Machine tack the frames in place, then quilt the frames and exposed foundation areas. Do not quilt the edge frames until after you have attached the binding to your quilt.

7. See "Finishing Your Quilt" on page 17 for making and attaching the binding. You will need a 2½"-wide binding strip at least 235" long. After the binding is attached, you can quilt the edge panes, then finish the binding by hand, stitching it to the back of your quilt.

Holiday Magic

Shelley Swanland, 2000, Cayucos, California, 20" x 36".

Holidays are a perfect time to display special quilts, and with its festive fabrics and central star motif, what could be more appropriate to hang on your wall or door than this "Holiday Magic" quilt? It requires only one block, so you may want to make two—one for you and one for gift giving.

Quilt Plan

Quilt Size: 20" x 36"
16" Morning Star block: Make 1.

Materials

	Fabric	Amount
Foundations	Snowflake print	³⁄₈ yd.
Frames	Dark green batik	³⁄₈ yd.
	Gold print	¹⁄₈ yd.
Panes	Floral Christmas print	¹⁄₃ yd.
	Holly print	¹⁄₈ yd.
Border 1	Floral Christmas print	³⁄₈ yd.
Border 2	Red Christmas print	¹⁄₄ yd.
Border 3	Dark green batik	¹⁄₄ yd.
Border 4	Snowflake print	¹⁄₄ yd.
Binding	Dark green batik	¹⁄₂ yd.
Backing		1 yd.
Batting		26" x 42"

Quilt Top Assembly

1. Following the instructions for the Morning Star block on page 48, make 1 block.

2. Pin the floral Christmas print template C-WP edge-kite panes in place.

3. Add the 16½"-long floral Christmas print border strips to the sides of the quilt.

4 Add a 20½"-long floral Christmas print border strip to the top and bottom of the quilt.

5. Using the red Christmas print, dark green batik, and snowflake print border pieces, follow the diagrams at right to construct 2 border units.

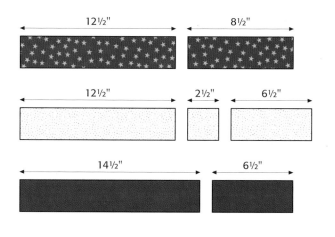

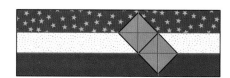

Cutting *Cut all pieces in the order listed below.*

Pieces	Fabric	First Cut	Second Cut
Foundations	Snowflake print	2 strips, 4½" x 42"	16 squares, 4½" x 4½"
Frames	Dark green batik	1 strip, 7⅛" x 42"	4 template A
		1 strip, 4" x 42"	4 template C
			4 template C reversed
		1 square, 4½" x 4½"	
		1 strip, 2½" x 42"	4 squares, 2½" x 2½"
	Gold print	1 strip, 4½" x 42"	8 squares, 4½" x 4½"
Panes	Floral Christmas print	1 strip, 3¼" x 42"	4 template A-WP
		1 strip, 2" x 42"	4 template C-WP
			4 template C-WP reversed
			1 square, 2" x 2"
		1 strip, 2½" x 6"	2 squares, 2½" x 2½"; cut both in half diagonally
	Holly print	1 strip, 2" x 42"	8 squares, 2" x 2"
Borders	Floral Christmas print	5 strips, 2½" x 42"	4 strips, 2½" x 20½"
			2 strips, 2½" x 16½"
	Red Christmas print	2 strips, 2½" x 42"	2 strips, 2½" x 12½"
			2 strips, 2½" x 8½"
	Dark green batik	2 strips, 2½" x 42"	2 strips, 2½" x 14½"
			2 strips, 2½" x 6½"
	Snowflake print	2 strips, 2½" x 42"	2 strips, 2½" x 12½"
			2 rectangles, 2½" x 6½"
			2 squares, 2½" x 2½"

6. Sew the pieced border units to the top and bottom of the quilt top.

7. Add the remaining 20½"-long floral Christmas print border strips to the top and bottom of the quilt.

8. Press the quilt top, referring to "Pressing" on page 15.

9. Trim the quilt backing so it measures approximately 26" x 42". Layer the batting, backing, and quilt top. Lay out the remaining window-panes and pin-baste through each pane and foundation unit, starting at the center of the quilt and working outward. Pin-baste the borders.

10. Machine tack the frames in place, then quilt the frames, foundations, and borders.

11. See "Finishing Your Quilt" on page 17 for making and attaching the binding. You will need a 2½"-wide binding strip at least 165" long.

PART FOUR

Introducing the Diamond Star, Creating Multiple Stars

The Diamond Star is dramatic yet simple. When you use diamond-shaped frames along the edges of the blocks in the previous section, you can create quilts with multiple stars. Once again, the difference in the patterns comes from the shapes you start with; the techniques are the same.

THE BLOCKS

DIAMOND STAR

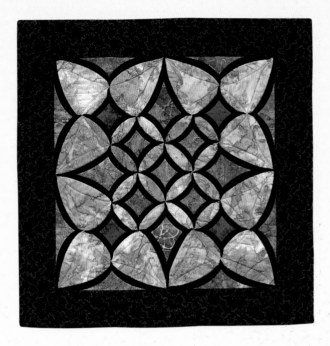

DIAMOND-EDGE CATHEDRAL STAR

DIAMOND-EDGE MORNING STAR

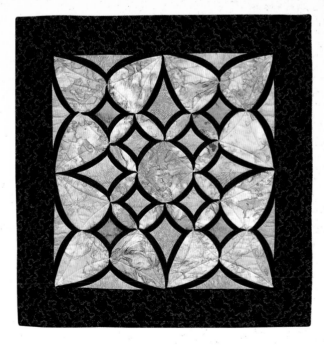

DIAMOND-EDGE TWILIGHT STAR

Diamond Star

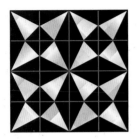

Foundation and Frame Grid

Pane Layout

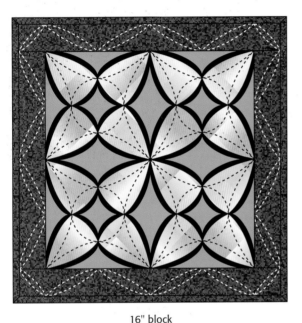

16" block

Block Assembly

This block uses only large foundation squares. Refer to "Sewing Diamond and Kite Frames Using Large Foundation Squares" on page 12.

1. Sew the long points of 4 black template B diamond frames together with 4 light batik 4½" foundation squares.

2. Sew the opposite long seams, adding 2 more light batik 4½" foundation squares to each.

3. As you complete the remaining seams of the diamond frame, add a black 4½" square frame in each corner. You will need another 4½" foundation square to complete each square frame.

4. As you sew the last 2 seams of the corner square frames, add the 8 black template D edge-diamond frames.

5. Cut 3"-wide strips for borders. Refer to "Butted Borders" on page 16. See "Finishing Your Quilt" on page 17 to add the windowpanes and complete your project.

Cutting

Pieces	Fabric	First Cut	Second Cut
Foundations	Light batik	2 strips, 4½" x 42"	16 squares, 4½" x 4½"
Frames	Black print	1 strip, 8¾" x 42"	4 template B
		2 strips, 4" x 42"	8 template D
		1 strip, 4½" x 42"	4 squares, 4½" x 4½"
Panes	Green print	1 strip, 2⅞" x 42"	4 template B-WP
		1 strip, 2" x 42"	8 template D-WP
			4 squares, 2" x 2"

Diamond-Edge Cathedral Star

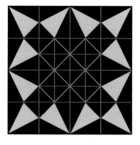

Foundation and Frame Grid

Pane Layout

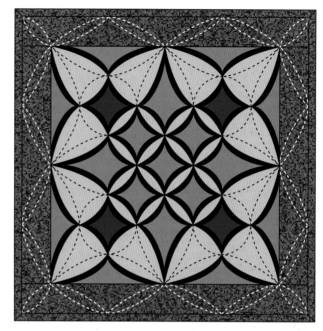

16" block

Cutting

Pieces	Fabric	First Cut	Second Cut
Foundations	Light batik	2 strips, 4½" x 42"	12 squares, 4½" x 4½"
		1 strip, 2½" x 42"	16 squares, 2½" x 2½"
Frames	Black print	1 strip, 7⅛" x 42"	4 template A
		2 strips, 4" x 42"	8 template D
		2 strips, 4½" x 42"	9 squares, 4½" x 4½"
Panes	Medium print	1 strip, 4¼" x 42"	4 template A-WP
		1 strip, 2" x 42"	8 template D-WP
		1 strip, 2" x 12"	5 squares, 2" x 2"
	Blue batik	1 strip, 2" x 12"	4 squares, 2" x 2"

Block Assembly

1. Construct a single square frame, using 1 black 4½" square frame and 4 light batik 2½" foundation squares and referring to "Sewing Square Frames" on page 9.

2. Add 1 more black 4½" square frame to each corner of the completed frame to create a 5-frame center unit. Refer to "Adding Additional Square Frames" on page 10.

3. Add 4 black template A kite frames one at a time, working around the center of the block.

4. Sew the opposite end of each kite frame, adding 2 light batik 4½" foundation squares to each.

5. As you complete the remaining seams of each kite frame, add a black 4½" square frame in each corner. You will need another large foundation square to complete each square frame.

6. As you sew the last 2 seams of each corner square frame, add the 8 template D edge-diamond frames to the block.

7. To turn your block into a small wall hanging, cut 3"-wide strips for borders. Refer to "Butted Borders" on page 16. See "Finishing Your Quilt" on page 17 to add the windowpanes and complete your project.

Diamond-Edge Morning Star

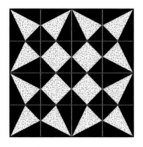

Foundation and Frame Grid

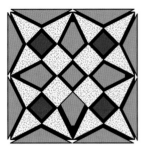

Pane Layout

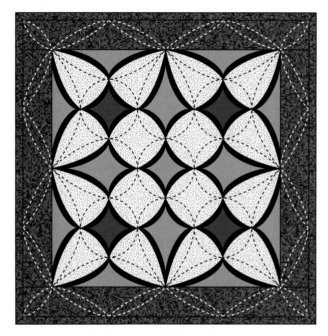

16" block

Cutting

Pieces	Fabric	First Cut	Second Cut
Foundations	Light batik	2 strips, 4½" x 42"	16 squares, 4½" x 4½"
Frames	Black solid	1 strip, 7⅛" x 42"	4 template A
		2 strips, 4" x 42"	8 template D
		1 strip, 4½" x 42"	5 squares, 4½" x 4½"
Panes	Pink batik	1 strip, 3¼" x 42"	4 template A-WP
		1 strip, 2" x 42"	8 template D-WP
		1 strip, 2" x 42"	5 squares, 2" x 2"

Block Assembly

This block uses only large foundation squares. Refer to "Sewing Diamond and Kite Frames Using Large Foundation Squares" on page 12.

1. Sew the short end of 4 black template A kite frames, tails pointing outward, around 1 black 4½" square frame, using 4 light batik 4½" foundation squares.

2. Sew the opposite end of each kite frame, using 2 light batik 4½" foundation squares for each.

3. As you complete the remaining seams of the kite frames, add a black 4½" square frame in each corner. You will need another 4½" foundation square to complete each square frame.

4. As you sew the last 2 seams of each corner square frame, add the 8 black template D edge-diamond frames to the block.

5. To turn your block into a small wall hanging, cut 3"-wide strips for borders. Refer to "Butted Borders" on page 16. See "Finishing Your Quilt" on page 17 to add the windowpanes and complete your project.

Diamond-Edge Twilight Star

Foundation and Frame Grid

Pane Layout

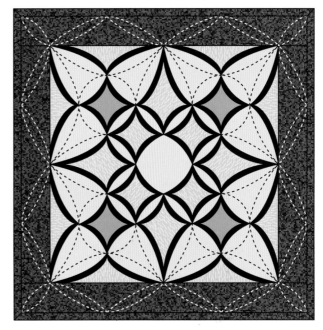

16" block

Cutting

Pieces	Fabric	First Cut	Second Cut
Foundations	Light multicolor batik	2 strips, 4½" x 42"	13 squares, 4½" x 4½"
		1 strip, 2½" x 42"	12 squares, 2½" x 2½"
Frames	Black print	1 strip, 7⅛" x 42"	4 template A
		2 strips, 4" x 42"	8 template D
		1 strip, 4½" x 42"	8 squares, 4½" x 4½"
Panes	Yellow batik	1 strip, 3¼" x 42"	4 template A-WP
		1 strip, 2" x 42"	8 template D-WP
		1 strip, 2" x 42"	8 squares, 2" x 2"

Block Assembly

1. Starting with a light multicolor batik 4½" foundation square in the center, add a black 4½" square frame and 3 light multicolor batik 2½" foundation squares to each corner.

2. Add a black template A kite frame to each side of the center unit.

3. Sew the opposite end of each kite frame, using 2 light multicolor batik 4½" foundation squares for each.

4. Sew the remaining seams of each kite frame.

5. Add a black 4½" square frame to each corner of the block. As you sew the last 2 seams of each square frame, add the 8 black template D edge-diamond frames.

6. To turn your block into a small wall hanging, cut 3"-wide strips for borders. Refer to "Butted Borders" on page 16. See "Finishing Your Quilt" on page 17 to add the windowpanes and complete your project.

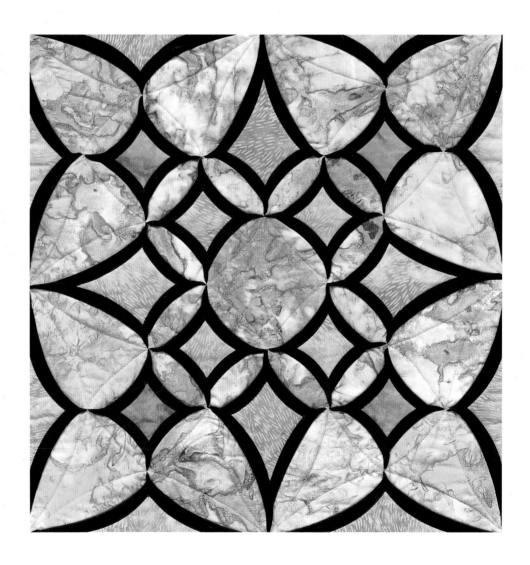

Exotic Diamond Star

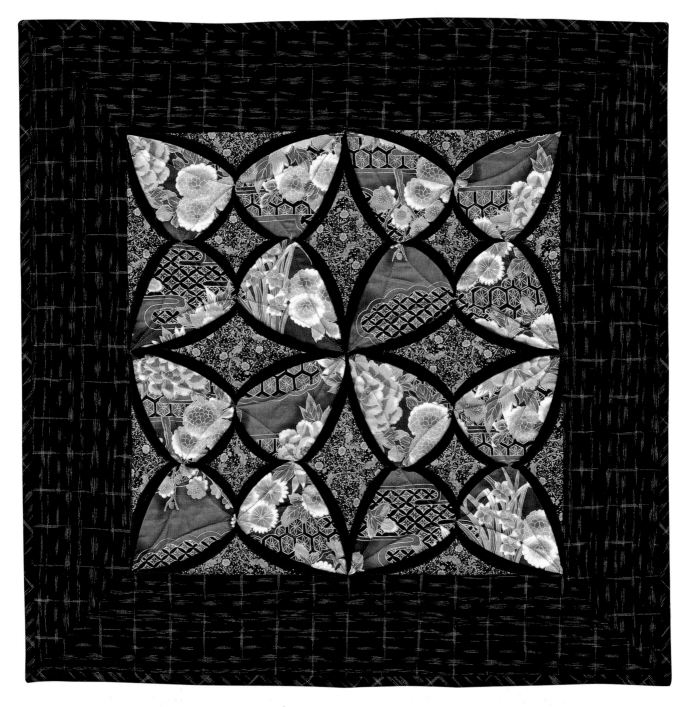

Shelley Swanland, 2000, Cayucos, California, 28" x 28".
The teardrop shape of the foundations in the Diamond Star design lends itself
to exotic fabrics, such as the Japanese-inspired fabric used here. Try your favorite
bold-print ethnic fabric, whether it's Asian, African, or Dutch. Other large-scale
prints will work equally well for a more traditional look.

Quilt Plan

Quilt Size: 28" x 28"
20" Diamond Star block: Make 1.

Materials

	Fabric	Amount
Foundations	Japanese floral print	⅝ yd.
Frames	Black solid	¾ yd.
Panes	Gray print	⅓ yd.
Borders and binding	Black print	1¼ yds.
Backing		1 yd.
Batting		34" x 34"

Cutting   *Cut all pieces in the order listed below.*

Pieces	Fabric	First Cut	Second Cut
Foundations	Japanese floral print	3 strips, 5½" x 42"	16 squares, 5½" x 5½"
Frames	Black solid	1 strip, 10¾" x 42"	4 template F
		2 strips, 4¾" x 42"	8 template H
		1 strip, 5½" x 42"	4 squares, 5½" x 5½"
Panes	Gray print	1 strip, 3⅝" x 42"	4 template F-WP
		2 strips, 2¼" x 42"	8 template H-WP
		1 strip, 2½" x 42"	4 squares, 2½" x 2½"
Borders	Black print	4 strips, 5½" x 42"	

Quilt Top Assembly

1. Following the instructions for the Diamond Star block on page 66, make 1 block.

2. Press the quilt top, referring to "Pressing" on page 15.

3. Pin the gray template H-WP edge-diamond panes in place.

4. Add the borders, referring to "Mitered Borders" on page 16.

5. Trim the quilt backing so it measures approximately 34" x 34". Layer the batting, backing, and quilt top. Lay out the windowpane squares. Pin-baste through each window and foundation, starting at the center of the quilt and working outward. Also pin-baste the borders.

6. Machine tack the frames in place, then quilt the frames, foundations, and border.

7. See "Finishing Your Quilt" on page 17 to make and attach the binding. You will need a 2½"-wide binding strip at least 140" long.

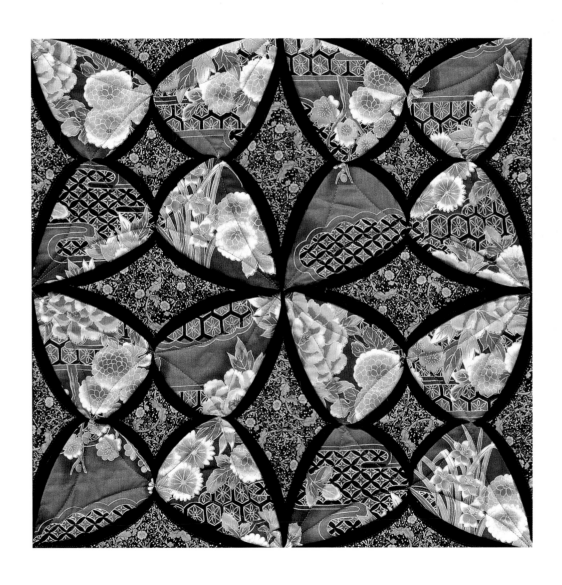

Autumn Stars

Shelley Swanland, 2000, Cayucos, California, 32½" x 32½".
The bright red and gold foundation fabrics in this quilt form a highly visible flowerlike pattern, while the more subdued colors of the autumn print windows recede to the background, making the Diamond Star design less prominent. Play with your color and fabric pattern choices to determine which part of the design you'd like to emphasize.

Quilt Plan

Quilt Size: 32½" x 32½"
16" Diamond Star block: Make 4.

Materials

	Fabric	Amount
Foundations	Gold print	⅝ yd.
	Red print	⅝ yd.
Frames	Black solid	2 yds.
Panes	Autumn print	⅝ yd.
Binding	Black solid	⅓ yd.
Backing		1⅛ yds.
Batting		36" x 36"

Cutting *Cut all pieces in the order listed below.*

Pieces	Fabric	First Cut	Second Cut
Foundations	Gold print	4 strips, 4½" x 42"	32 squares, 4½" x 4½"
	Red print	4 strips, 4½" x 42"	32 squares, 4½" x 4½"
Frames	Black solid	5 strips, 8¾" x 42"	24 template B
		3 strips, 4" x 42"	16 template D
		2 strips, 4½" x 42"	16 squares, 4½" x 4½"
Panes	Autumn print	3 strips, 2⅞" x 42"	24 template B-WP
		2 strips, 2" x 42"	16 template D-WP
		1 strip, 2" x 42"	16 squares, 2" x 2"

Quilt Top Assembly

1. Following the instructions for the Diamond Star block on page 66, make 4 blocks without the edge frames. Use the red 4½" foundation squares for the 4 block centers and 4 corners. The remaining 8 foundation squares in each block are gold.

2. Lay out the 4 blocks. Where each block meets another block, connect the blocks by constructing 2 diamond frames. You'll need a total of 8 diamond frames.

3. Add 4 black template D edge-diamond frames to each side of the quilt top.

4. Press the quilt top, referring to "Pressing" on page 15.

5. Trim the quilt backing so it measures approximately 36" x 36". Layer the batting, backing, and quilt top. Lay out the windowpanes and pin-baste them in place through all layers. Also pin-baste through the foundation areas, starting at the center of the quilt and working outward.

6. Machine tack the frames in place, then quilt the frames and foundations. Don't quilt the edge frames yet. Wait until the binding has been attached before quilting them.

7. See "Finishing Your Quilt" on page 17 for making and attaching the binding. You will need a 2½"-wide binding strip at least 142" long. After you have attached the binding to the front of the quilt, quilt the edge panes. Then fold the binding to the back of the quilt and stitch in place.

Star Sampler

Shelley Swanland, 2000, Cayucos, California, 46" x 46". Quilted by Gwen Weedon.
Individual blocks really shine when separated by sashing in a muted shade. Here, the
blocks are treated just as in any other traditional patchwork quilt: four different blocks are
separated by sashing, stitched together as a sampler quilt, and surrounded by a large-scale floral
print border. I'm sure you'll agree that the result is anything but typical!

Quilt Plan

Quilt Size: 46" x 46"
16" Diamond Star block,
16" Diamond-Edge Cathedral Star block,
16" Diamond Edge Morning Star block,
16" Diamond-Edge Twilight Star block: Make 1 each.

Materials

	Fabric	Amount
Foundations	Rosebud print	1⅜ yds.
Frames	White print	1⅞ yds.
Panes	Rose print	½ yd.
Panes and sashing	Green print	⅞ yd.
Borders and binding	Rose print	1½ yds.
Backing		3 yds.
Batting		52" x 52"

Cutting *Cut all pieces in the order listed below.*

Pieces	Fabric	First Cut	Second Cut
Foundations	Rosebud print	8 strips, 4½" x 42"	57 squares, 4½" x 4½"
		2 strips, 2½" x 42"	28 squares, 2½" x 2½"
Frames	White print	1 strip, 8¾" x 42"	4 template B
		2 strips, 7⅛" x 42"	12 template A
		4 strips, 4½" x 42"	26 squares, 4½" x 4½"
		5 strips, 4" x 42"	32 template D
Panes	Rose print	1 strip, 2⅞" x 42"	4 template B-WP
		1 strip, 3¼" x 42"	12 template A-WP
		2 strips, 2½" x 42"	26 squares, 2" x 2"
	Green print	4 strips, 2" x 42"	32 template D-WP
Sashing	Green print	6 strips, 2½" x 42"	2 strips, 2½" x 16½"
			3 strips, 2½" x 34½"
			2 strips, 2½" x 38½"
Borders	Rose print	4½" wide, cut lengthwise	

Quilt Top Assembly

1. Assemble 1 of each block: Diamond Star (see page 66), Diamond-Edge Cathedral Star (see page 67), Diamond-Edge Morning Star (see page 68), and Diamond-Edge Twilight Star (see page 71), including edge frames on all blocks. Press the blocks, referring to "Pressing" on page 15.

2. Pin the green template D-WP edge-diamond panes in place on each block, then sew the sashing strips to the blocks as shown below. Join the blocks together.

3. Attach the borders, referring to "Mitered Borders" on page 15.

4. Press the quilt top, referring to "Pressing" on page 15.

5. Piece the quilt backing so it measures approximately 52" x 52". Layer the batting, backing, and quilt top. Lay out the windowpanes and pin-baste them in place. Also pin-baste through each frame and foundation, through all layers, starting at the center of the quilt and working outward. Pin-baste the sashing and borders.

6. Machine tack the frames in place, then quilt the frames, foundations, sashing, and borders. The sashing needs to be quilted fairly heavily to balance the amount of quilting in the blocks.

7. See "Finishing Your Quilt" on page 17 for making and attaching the binding. You will need a 2½"-wide binding strip at least 204" long.

A Window Full of Stars

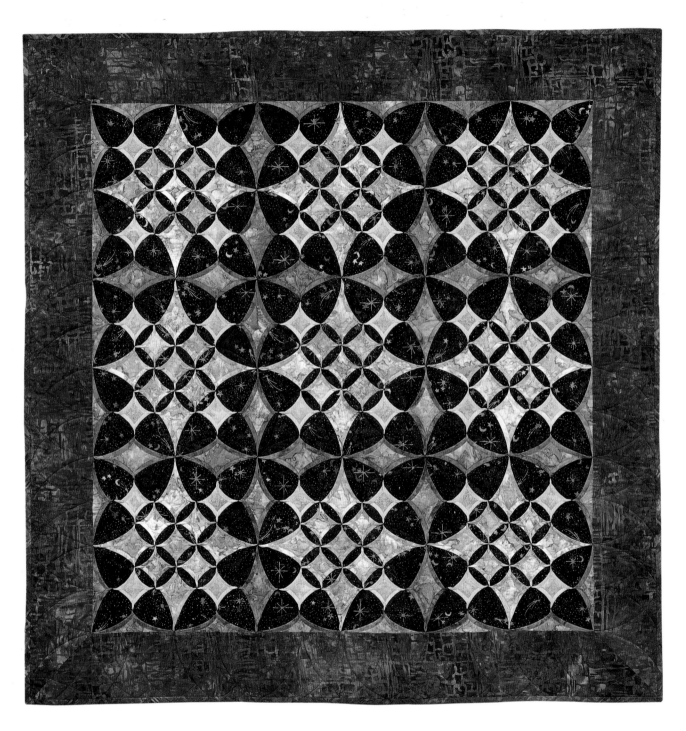

Shelley Swanland, 2000, Cayucos, California, 60" x 60".
This beautiful design is reminiscent of a stained-glass rose window, with its soft lavender
stars set against a nighttime sky of dark circles. The yellow fabric contrasts nicely with
the purple and other pastel hues for an overall stunning effect.

Quilt Plan

Quilt Size: 60" x 60"
16" Diamond-Edge Cathedral Star block: Make 9.

Materials

	Fabric	Amount
Foundations	Black celestial batik	2⅝ yds.
Frames	Yellow batik	2⅛ yds.
	Purple batik	1⅞ yds.
	Yellow solid	⅞ yd.
Panes	Light orange batik	¼ yd.
	Light purple batik	⅝ yd.
Borders and binding	Purple batik	2½ yds.
Backing		4 yds.
Batting		66" x 66"

Cutting   *Cut all pieces in the order listed below.*

Pieces	Fabric	First Cut	Second Cut
Foundations	Black celestial batik	14 strips, 4½" x 42"	108 squares, 4½" x 4½"
		9 strips, 2½" x 42"	144 squares, 2½" x 2½"
Frames	Yellow batik	6 strips, 7⅛" x 42"	36 template A
		6 strips, 4½" x 42"	45 squares, 4½" x 4½"
	Purple batik	5 strips, 8¾" x 42"	24 template B
		4 strips, 4" x 42"	24 template D
	Yellow solid	5 strips, 4½" x 42"	36 squares, 4½" x 4½"
Panes	Light orange batik	2 strips, 2" x 42"	36 squares, 2" x 2"
	Light purple batik	3 strips, 2⅞" x 42"	24 template B-WP
		3 strips, 2" x 42"	24 template D-WP
Borders	Purple batik	4 strips, 6½" x 66", cut lengthwise	

Quilt Top Assembly

1. Following the instructions for the Diamond-Edge Cathedral Star block on page 67, make 9 blocks without adding the edge panes.

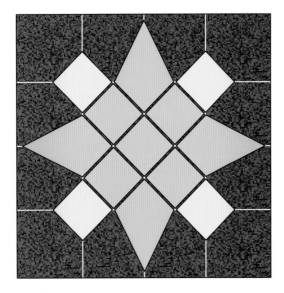

2. Lay out the 9 blocks. As you sew the blocks together, add 2 purple template B diamond frames at each side.

3. Sew 6 purple template D edge-diamond frames to each side of the quilt top.

4. Press the quilt top, referring to "Pressing" on page 15.

5. Pin the light purple template D-WP edge-diamond panes in place, then attach the borders, referring to "Mitered Borders" on page 15.

6. Piece the quilt backing so it measures approximately 66" x 66". Layer the batting, backing, and quilt top. Lay out the windowpanes. (Note: The yellow multibatik frames do not have panes.) Pin-baste through the windowpanes and foundations, through all layers, starting at the center of the quilt and working outward.

7. Machine tack the frames in place, then quilt the frames, foundations, and border.

8. See "Finishing Your Quilt" on page 17 for making and attaching the binding. You will need a 2½"-wide binding strip at least 250" long.

Patterns

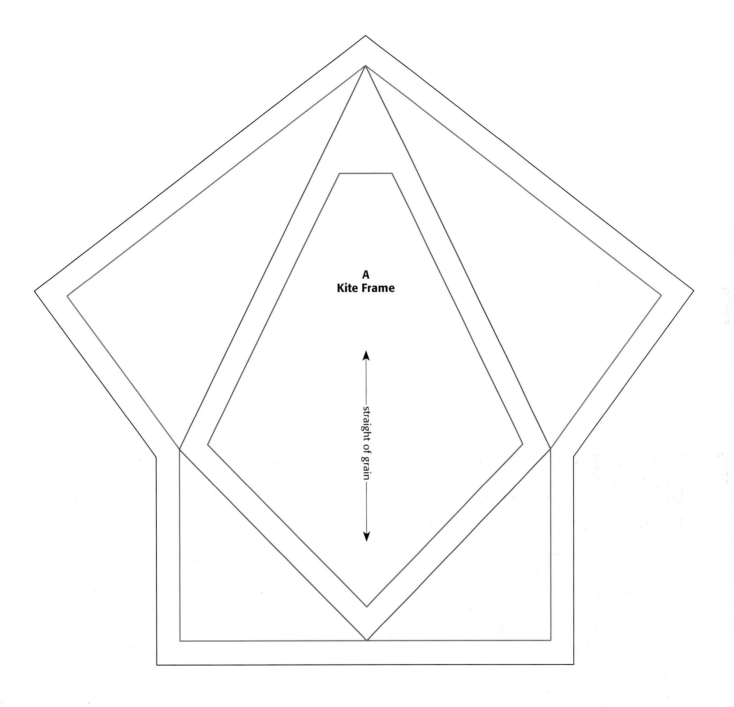

**A
Kite Frame**

straight of grain

Pane placement

Finished-frame folded edges

Seam line

Cutting line

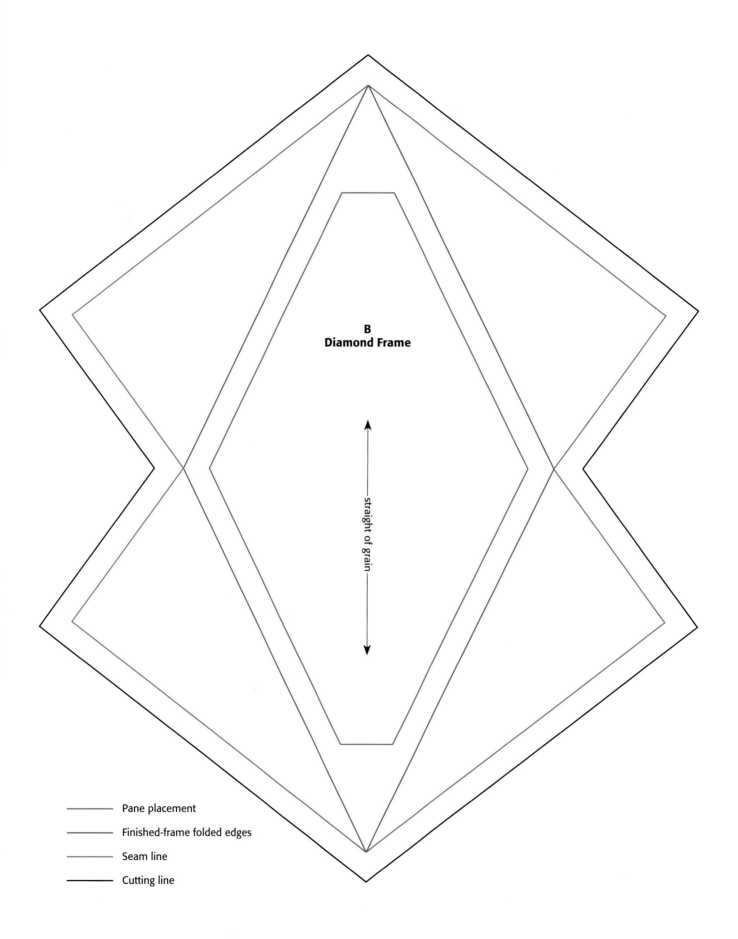

B
Diamond Frame

straight of grain

Pane placement

Finished-frame folded edges

Seam line

Cutting line

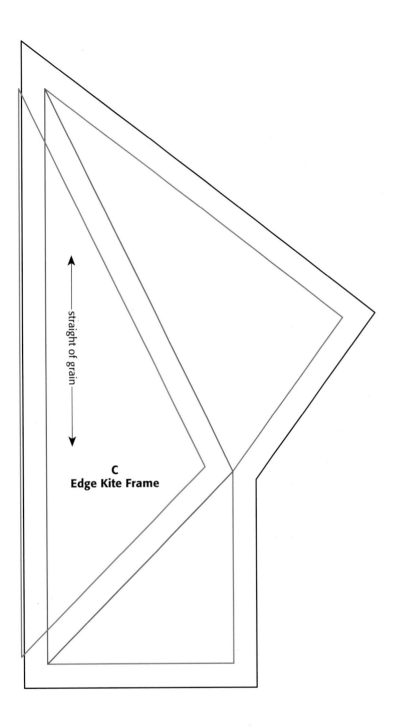

straight of grain

C
Edge Kite Frame

	Pane placement
	Finished-frame folded edges
	Seam line
	Cutting line

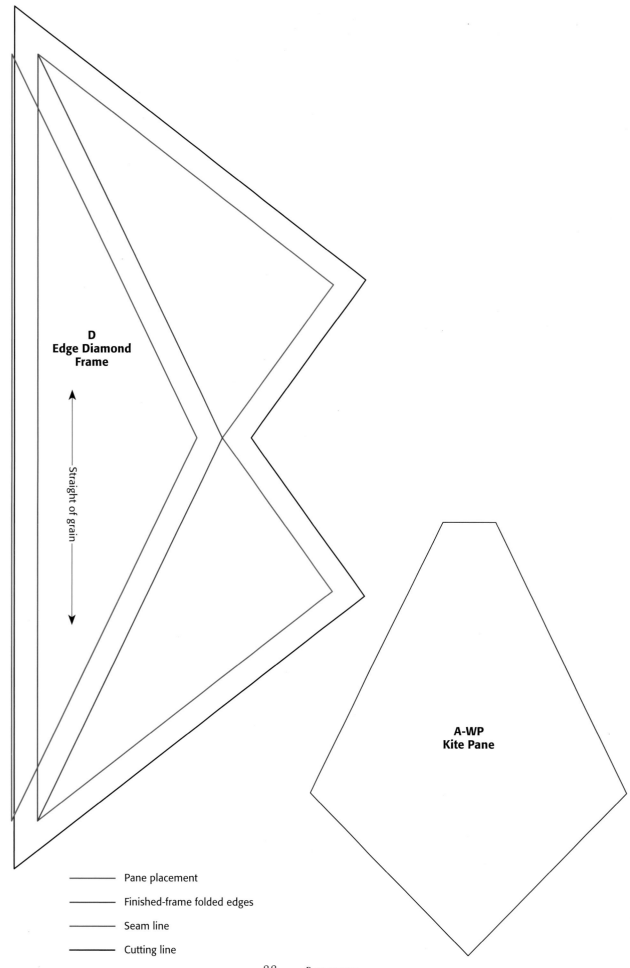

D
Edge Diamond
Frame

Straight of grain

A-WP
Kite Pane

Pane placement

Finished-frame folded edges

Seam line

Cutting line

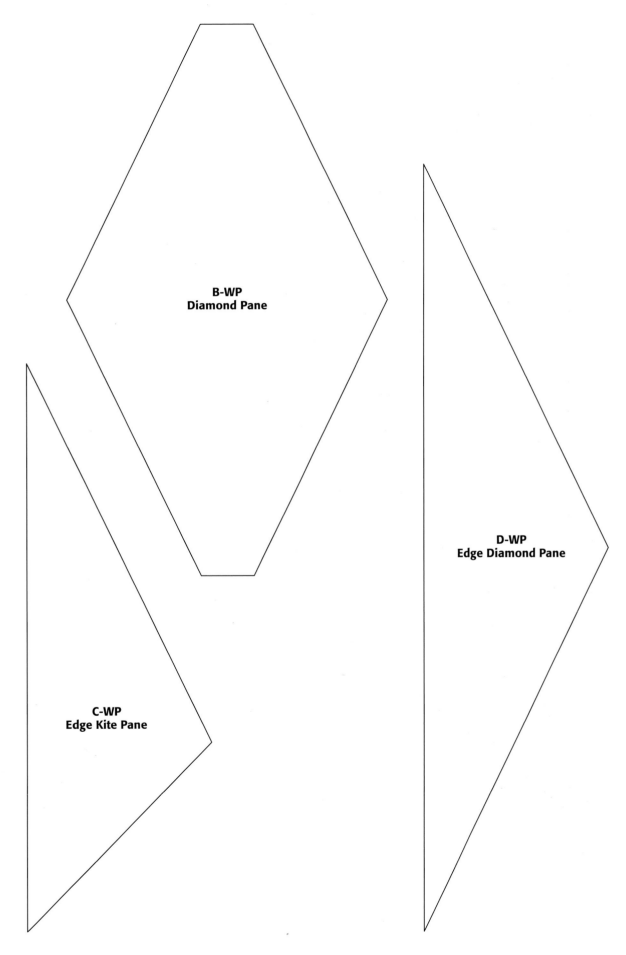

B-WP
Diamond Pane

C-WP
Edge Kite Pane

D-WP
Edge Diamond Pane

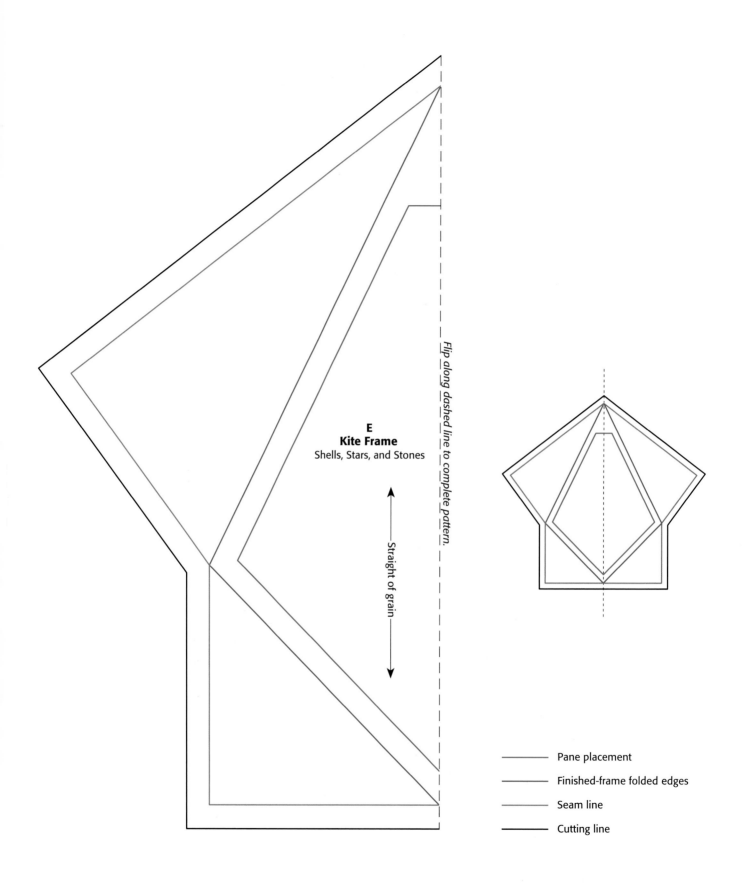

**E
Kite Frame**
Shells, Stars, and Stones

Flip along dashed line to complete pattern.

Straight of grain

Pane placement

Finished-frame folded edges

Seam line

Cutting line

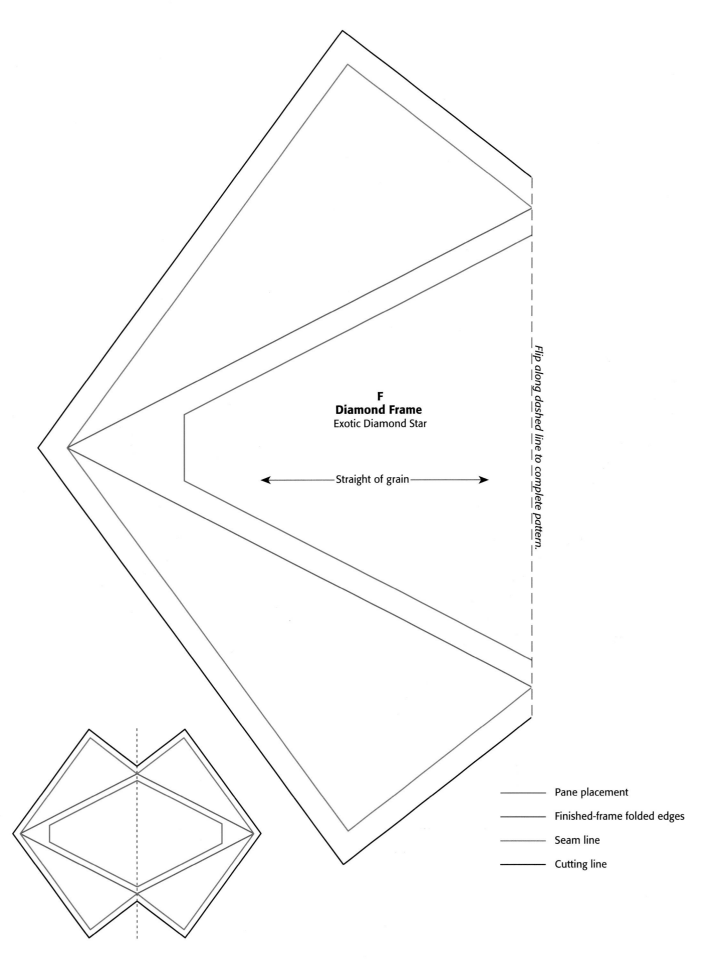

F
Diamond Frame
Exotic Diamond Star

Straight of grain

Flip along dashed line to complete pattern.

Pane placement

Finished-frame folded edges

Seam line

Cutting line

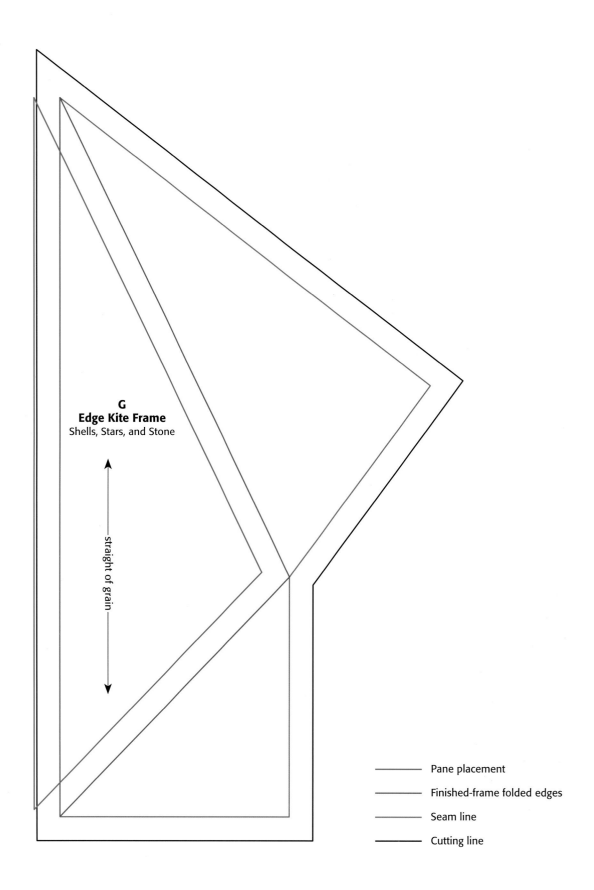

G
Edge Kite Frame
Shells, Stars, and Stone

straight of grain

Pane placement

Finished-frame folded edges

Seam line

Cutting line

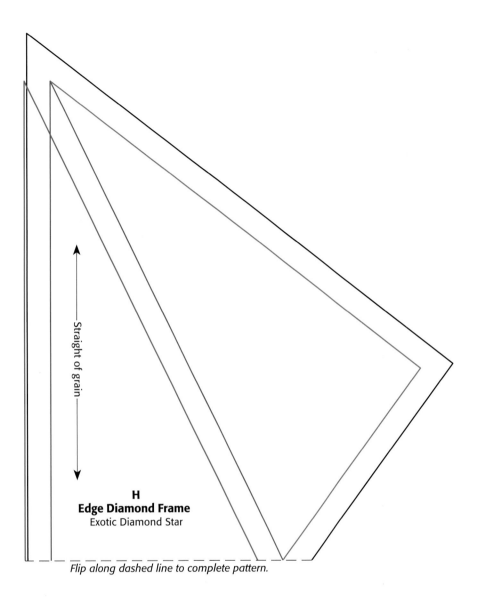

Straight of grain

H
Edge Diamond Frame
Exotic Diamond Star

Flip along dashed line to complete pattern.

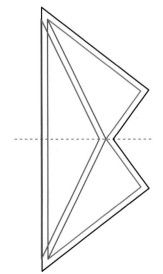

—— Pane placement

—— Finished-frame folded edges

—— Seam line

—— Cutting line

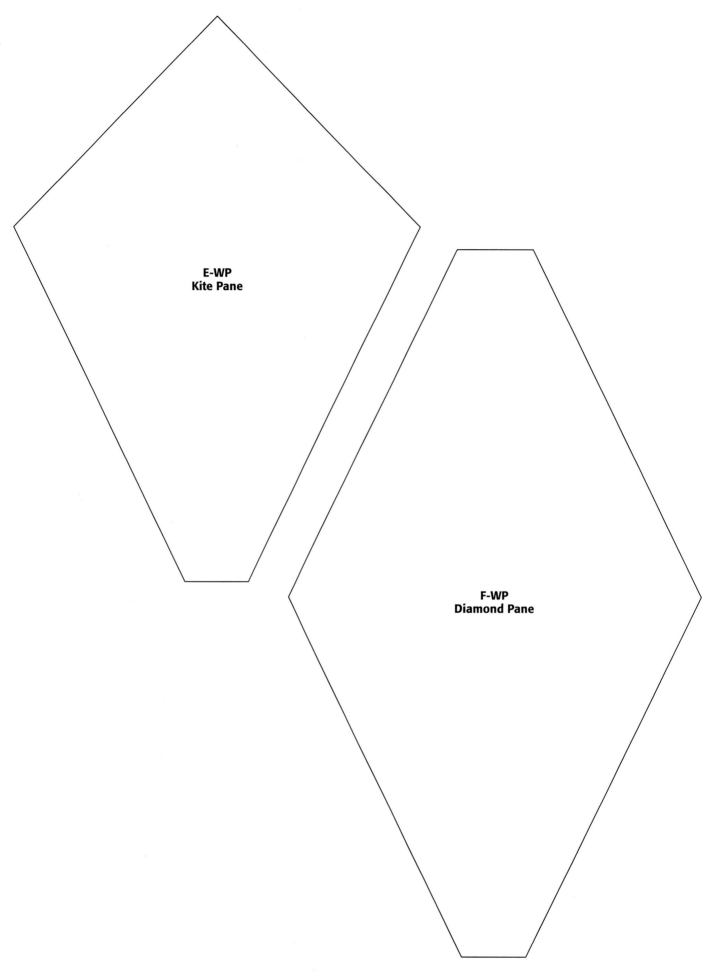

E-WP
Kite Pane

F-WP
Diamond Pane

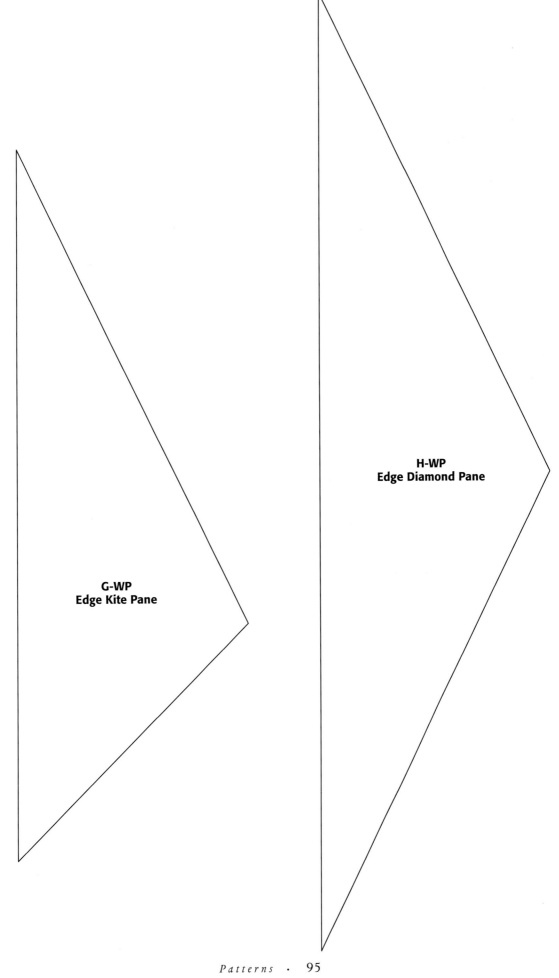

**G-WP
Edge Kite Pane**

**H-WP
Edge Diamond Pane**

7/02

out the Author

SEWING, QUILTING, and embroidery are Shelley Swanland's passions. Author of *Machine-Stitched Cathedral Windows,* published by Martingale & Company in 1999, Shelley also shares her technique for making Cathedral Window quilts through lectures, classes, and television programs. She makes her home on the central coast of California.